Shut Up and Build Muscle

Outrageously Tasty Low–Calorie, High–Protein Meals for High-Energy Living

BY

Jax Iron

No Fluff, Just Gains:
Why This Book Doesn't Need Pictures

Let's get something straight: **this isn't a book for scrolling through pretty pictures of food**. You won't find glossy, perfectly lit photos of plates you'll never recreate. Why? Because this book is about **results**, not aesthetics. It's about getting you shredded, fueled, and unstoppable—not flipping through pages like it's a coffee table magazine for foodies.

No distractions, no fluff—just the hard-hitting tools you need to dominate your goals. This isn't for kids who need colorful pictures to hold their attention. This is for people who are serious about crushing it in the gym, in the kitchen, and in life. If you need a photo to figure out how to make a chicken breast taste good, this book probably isn't for you anyway.

Here's the deal: **real progress isn't pretty.** It's messy meal prep containers, a fridge stocked with the essentials, and a pile of recipes that actually get the job done. This book doesn't need photos to prove its worth—every recipe, every chapter speaks for itself. You're here for gains, for fuel, for solutions, not for Instagram-worthy snapshots.

So if you're ready to **focus on what actually matters**, you're in the right place. This is a no-nonsense approach to building muscle, leaning out, and making food that works as hard as you do. **No photos needed.**

Shut Up and Build Muscle Written by Jax Iron

Published by Amazon.com 410 Terry Avenue North Seattle, WA 98109-5210, USA

INDEX

CHAPTER 1: SHUT UP AND START LIFTING

Stop whining and start winning—that's the core mantra you need to adopt right now. This book isn't here to hold your hand or serve up half-baked promises; it's a battle plan designed to get you off your butt and into the gym, armed with the right mindset and the right fuel. If you're tired of lame excuses, watered-down advice, and bland-as-hell diets, you've come to the right place. We're here to hammer home exactly what it takes to build muscle, crank up your energy levels, and keep you laser-focused on every rep.

But guess what? Your training is only half the story. You can hammer out a thousand push-ups or squat until your quads beg for mercy, yet if your diet sucks, you'll never see the results you crave. That's where our **200 recipes** come storming in: they're engineered to make your body a powerhouse without burning a hole in your taste buds. Think flavor-packed, high-protein, low-calorie meals that give you the edge you need—no time wasted on fluff or complicated cooking procedures.

So how do you make the most of it? First, ditch the victim mentality. Stop complaining that you're "too busy," "too tired," or "too new to this." Everyone starts somewhere, and trust me, no one's going to do the work for you. Next, set your eyes on the prize. Whether you want to pack on lean mass, shred excess fat, or simply stop feeling like a zombie every afternoon, this approach works—provided you show up and put in the effort.

In the chapters ahead, we'll tear down every excuse in the book. We'll talk about stocking your kitchen so you're never left rummaging for half-stale cereal. We'll break down macros in a way that doesn't make you want to gouge your eyes out. We'll hand you breakfast, lunch, dinner, and snack ideas so you never slip into a sad mealtime rut. And yeah, we'll even tackle cheat meals—because sometimes you need to treat yourself without completely derailing your progress.

The bottom line? **This book is your fast-track ticket** to building serious muscle and fueling your body like the machine it's meant to be. You bring the grit and determination. We'll bring the recipes and strategies. Together, we'll knock down every barrier between you and the results you've been dying to see.

Ready to level up? Good. Flip the page, because it's time to shut up and start lifting. Your excuses called in sick, and your future self is counting on you to show up strong. Let's do this.

CHAPTER 2: KITCHEN SURVIVAL 101: STOCK UP OR SHUT UP

From protein powerhouses to essential spices, this chapter shows you exactly what you need in your pantry to churn out muscle-fueling meals in no time.

You can squat a small car, but if your fridge and cupboards look like a trash heap of stale crackers and expired sauces, you're shooting your gains in the foot—hard. Don't blame "bad genetics" or your "busy schedule" when you can't even be bothered to keep a proper stash of muscle-building essentials on deck. This chapter tears down the barriers between you and a kitchen that's primed to pump out lean, flavorful meals without the last-minute scramble.

From Protein Powerhouses to Spice-Rack Magic

First up: **protein**. You want size and strength? Load up on **chicken breasts**, **lean ground turkey**, **fish**, **egg whites**, or **plant-based staples** like **tofu** and **tempeh**. No more whining about "no time to cook" when you've got freezer bags full of ready-to-go protein. Next, **spices**—and I don't mean a sad shaker of salt and pepper. Get the likes of **garlic powder**, **paprika**, **chili flakes**, **Italian seasoning**, and **cumin** on your shelf, so you can blast flavor into every meal without drowning it in junk calories.

Carbs, Fats, and the Right Tools

Don't fall for the carb-hate hype. **Complex carbs**—brown rice, quinoa, oats—keep your energy tank from hitting empty halfway through your workout. Pair them with **healthy fats** like **avocados**, **nuts**, and **seeds** to stabilize hormones and keep your body humming along. And yes, you'll need the right hardware: a **non-stick pan** that won't turn your chicken breast into rubber, a **sharp-ass knife** that makes meal prep a breeze, and a set of **meal-prep containers** to stash your food for the week.

No More Excuses

Let's be real: if you're still blaming your fridge for your lack of progress, you're not in this for real. By the end of this chapter, you'll know exactly what you need in your pantry—and why. Stock up, prep smart, and watch your workouts and meals hit a new gear. Or keep complaining and settle for a half-baked diet that leaves your body lagging behind. Your call.

Ready to stop making excuses and start making gains? Good. Flip the page, and let's set your kitchen up to fuel the kind of results you've been dying to see. Because in this game, victory favors the **well-prepared**, and it all starts here.

Recipes Included: About 15 Basics for Sauces, Seasonings, and Protein Staples

So you've got your pantry stacked, your tools sharpened—now it's time to actually **cook**. Below is a sneak peek at **15 foundational recipes** that'll lay the groundwork for flavor-packed, muscle-fueling meals. Think of these as your go-to building blocks: whip 'em up in batches, store 'em smart, and pull 'em out whenever you need a quick punch of protein or a blast of seasonings to turn bland into badass.

1. **Hot & Smoky Chipotle Rub**
   - **Why It Rocks**: Adds bold flavor with minimal calories; perfect for grilled chicken, fish, tofu, or even roasted veggies.
   - **Ingredients** (makes about 1 cup of rub):
     1. 2 tbsp chipotle powder
     2. 2 tbsp smoked paprika
     3. 1 tbsp garlic powder
     4. 1 tbsp onion powder
     5. 1 tsp cayenne pepper (or less if you're not a heat freak)
     6. 1 tbsp salt
     7. 1 tbsp ground black pepper
   - **Method**:
     1. Combine all the spices in a small bowl or jar.
     2. Stir or shake well until evenly mixed.
     3. Store in an airtight container for up to 3 months.
   - **Pro Tip**: Rub it generously onto proteins (or veggies) about 15–30 minutes before cooking. Let the flavors sink in—then grill, bake, or sauté to let the heat and smoke do their thing.

2. **Zesty Lemon-Garlic Marinade**
   - **Why It Rocks**: Bright, tangy, and a total game-changer for bland chicken or fish.
   - **Ingredients** (enough for about 1–1.5 lbs of protein):
     1. ¼ cup freshly squeezed lemon juice
     2. 2 tbsp olive oil (don't worry; you're dividing it across multiple servings)
     3. 3 cloves garlic, minced (or 1 tbsp garlic paste)
     4. 1 tsp dried oregano
     5. ½ tsp salt
     6. ¼ tsp black pepper
   - **Method**:
     1. Whisk all ingredients in a bowl or pour into a zip-top bag.

2. Add your protein (chicken breasts, fish fillets, tofu, etc.) and let it marinate for at least 30 minutes, up to 2 hours.
3. Cook using your preferred method—grill, bake, or pan-sear.

Pro Tip: Don't marinate delicate fish too long or it'll go mushy. For chicken, overnight in the fridge means flavor city.

3. **No-BS Herbed Chicken Breast**
   - **Why It Rocks**: Goodbye cardboard chicken. This one stays juicy and is stupid simple.
   - **Ingredients** (serves 3–4):
     1. 4 chicken breasts, ~6 oz each
     2. 2 tbsp olive oil
     3. 1 tsp dried thyme
     4. 1 tsp dried basil
     5. 1 tsp dried rosemary
     6. 1 tsp garlic powder
     7. 1 tsp salt
     8. ½ tsp pepper
   - **Method**:
     1. Preheat your oven to 400°F (200°C).
     2. Toss chicken breasts in olive oil and spices.
     3. Place on a baking sheet lined with foil or parchment.
     4. Bake for 20–25 minutes (depending on thickness) until juices run clear or internal temp is 165°F (74°C).
   - **Pro Tip**: Let it rest 5 minutes before slicing—locks in the juices so you're not chewing on rubber.

4. **Savage Teriyaki Sauce**
   - **Why It Rocks**: Sticky, sweet, and just enough heat to keep things interesting.
   - **Ingredients** (makes about 1 cup):
     1. ½ cup low-sodium soy sauce (or tamari for gluten-free)
     2. ¼ cup water
     3. 2 tbsp honey (or maple syrup)
     4. 1 tbsp rice vinegar
     5. 1 clove garlic, minced
     6. 1 tsp minced fresh ginger (or ½ tsp dried ginger)
     7. 1 tsp cornstarch + 1 tbsp water (slurry)
     8. Pinch of red chili flakes (optional)
   - **Method**:
     1. Combine soy sauce, water, honey, vinegar, garlic, ginger, and chili flakes in a saucepan.
     2. Bring to a simmer over medium heat.

3. Stir in cornstarch slurry and keep stirring until sauce thickens—about 1–2 minutes.
4. Remove from heat.
- **Pro Tip**: Baste onto chicken thighs, salmon fillets, or even tofu in the last few minutes of cooking. Reserve some on the side for dipping—but don't use the raw marinade as a sauce!

5. **Overnight Steak Marinade**
   - **Why It Rocks**: Takes a lean cut from mediocre to mouthwatering.
   - **Ingredients** (enough for 1–2 lbs of steak):
     1. ¼ cup low-sodium soy sauce
     2. 2 tbsp Worcestershire sauce
     3. 1 tbsp Dijon mustard
     4. 2 cloves garlic, crushed
     5. 1 tsp black pepper
     6. 1 tbsp olive oil
   - **Method**:
     1. Whisk all ingredients in a bowl or zip-top bag.
     2. Add steak, seal, and marinate in the fridge overnight.
     3. Grill, broil, or pan-sear to your preferred doneness.
   - **Pro Tip**: Let the steak rest at least 5 minutes after cooking, so the juices redistribute (aka no sad, dry steak).

6. **Garlic-Herb Tofu Crumble**
   - **Why It Rocks**: Tofu gets a bad rap—until you do it right. Crumble form = huge surface area for flavor.
   - **Ingredients** (serves 2–3):
     1. 1 block firm or extra-firm tofu, drained
     2. 1 tbsp olive oil
     3. 2 cloves garlic, minced
     4. 1 tsp dried basil or oregano
     5. ½ tsp salt
     6. ¼ tsp pepper
   - **Method**:
     1. Crumble tofu into a bowl. Use your hands; get messy.
     2. Heat oil in a non-stick skillet over medium-high heat.
     3. Sauté garlic until fragrant, ~1 minute.
     4. Add tofu, herbs, salt, and pepper. Cook until slightly browned and crispy, ~8–10 minutes.
   - **Pro Tip**: Serve it on salads, in wraps, or alongside roasted veggies for a protein boost that doesn't taste like sponge.

7. **Sriracha Honey Glaze**
   - **Why It Rocks**: Perfect balance of heat and sweet for wings, thighs, or even veggie kabobs.
   - **Ingredients** (makes ~¾ cup):
     1. ¼ cup honey
     2. 2 tbsp sriracha (more if you're a spice fiend)
     3. 1 tbsp soy sauce
     4. 1 tbsp rice vinegar
     5. 1 clove garlic, grated (optional)
   - **Method**:
     1. Whisk all ingredients in a small bowl.
     2. Brush onto protein or veggies in the last 5 minutes of cooking, or toss everything in a bowl after it's cooked.
   - **Pro Tip**: If you want a thicker glaze, simmer everything for a few minutes on the stove until it reduces.

8. **Basic Tomato Sauce with a Punch**
   - **Why It Rocks**: Better than any store-bought jar. You control the salt, sugar, and spice.
   - **Ingredients** (makes about 3 cups):
     1. 1 tbsp olive oil
     2. 1 small onion, finely chopped
     3. 2 cloves garlic, minced
     4. 1 can (28 oz) crushed tomatoes (low-sodium if possible)
     5. 1 tsp chili flakes (optional but recommended)
     6. 1 tsp dried basil (or Italian seasoning)
     7. Salt & pepper to taste
   - **Method**:
     1. Sauté onion in oil over medium heat until translucent, ~5 minutes.
     2. Add garlic (and chili flakes), cook 1 minute.
     3. Stir in tomatoes and basil. Simmer for 15–20 minutes, stirring occasionally.
     4. Season with salt and pepper.
   - **Pro Tip**: If you like it smoother, hit it with an immersion blender. Great for pasta, meatballs, or as a base for healthy pizzas.

9. **DIY Taco Seasoning**
   - **Why It Rocks**: No mystery fillers or crazy sodium levels.
   - **Ingredients** (makes a small jar, ~¼ cup):
     1. 1 tbsp chili powder
     2. 1 tsp cumin
     3. 1 tsp paprika
     4. 1 tsp garlic powder
     5. 1 tsp onion powder

6. ½ tsp dried oregano
7. ½ tsp salt (add more to taste)
8. ¼ tsp black pepper
- **Method**:
  1. Mix all ingredients in a small jar.
  2. Use ~1–2 tbsp per pound of ground meat (or veggie equivalent) when cooking.
- **Pro Tip**: For an extra kick, throw in a pinch of cayenne. Adjust salt based on your dietary needs and taste buds.

10. **Simple Baked Tempeh Strips**
- **Why It Rocks**: A crunchy, protein-packed alternative to bacon.
- **Ingredients** (serves 2–3):
  1. 1 package tempeh (8–10 oz)
  2. 2 tbsp soy sauce
  3. 1 tbsp maple syrup
  4. 1 tsp smoked paprika (optional but awesome)
- **Method**:
  1. Preheat oven to 375°F (190°C).
  2. Slice tempeh into thin strips.
  3. Mix soy sauce, maple syrup, and paprika in a small bowl.
  4. Dip tempeh strips in the mixture, place on a baking sheet lined with parchment.
  5. Bake 15–20 minutes, flipping halfway, until crisp.
- **Pro Tip**: These store great in the fridge. Reheat quickly in a skillet or microwave for a bacon-ish crunch on salads or sandwiches.

11. **All-Purpose Spice Blend**
- **Why It Rocks**: One jar to rule them all—great on chicken, veggies, even eggs.
- **Ingredients** (makes ~¼ cup):
  1. 1 tbsp salt
  2. 1 tbsp black pepper
  3. 1 tbsp garlic powder
  4. 1 tbsp onion powder
  5. 1 tbsp paprika
- **Method**:
  1. Combine everything in a small jar. Shake it like you mean it.
  2. Store up to 6 months.
- **Pro Tip**: Keep a shaker of this on the counter. Sprinkle on anything that needs a quick flavor boost.

12. **One-Skillet Protein Crumble**
- **Why It Rocks**: Easy as hell—great for tacos, bowls, wraps, you name it.
- **Ingredients** (makes ~4 servings):

1. 1 lb ground turkey or chicken
2. 1 small onion, diced
3. 1 bell pepper, diced
4. 1–2 tbsp of your favorite seasoning (Taco, All-Purpose, etc.)
- **Method**:
    1. Heat a non-stick skillet over medium-high.
    2. Sauté onion and pepper until slightly tender.
    3. Add ground meat and seasoning, cook until browned and fully done.
- **Pro Tip**: Make a double batch and freeze half. You've instantly got a pre-cooked protein option when life gets hectic.

13. **Kick-Ass Greek Yogurt Dip**
- **Why It Rocks**: High-protein alternative to mayo or sour cream.
- **Ingredients** (makes ~1.5 cups):
    1. 1 cup plain Greek yogurt
    2. 1 clove garlic, finely minced
    3. ½ cup cucumber, grated and squeezed dry (if you want a tzatziki vibe)
    4. 1 tbsp lemon juice
    5. ½ tsp salt
    6. ½ tsp dried dill or parsley (optional)
- **Method**:
    1. Stir all ingredients together in a bowl.
    2. Let it chill in the fridge for at least 15 minutes for flavors to meld.
- **Pro Tip**: Use it as a dipping sauce, a salad dressing, or a spread for wraps instead of calorie-bomb condiments.

14. **Lean Turkey Meatballs**
- **Why It Rocks**: Satisfies that comfort-food craving without the guilt.
- **Ingredients** (makes ~15 meatballs):
    1. 1 lb ground turkey (93% lean or better)
    2. 1 egg white
    3. ¼ cup breadcrumbs (whole wheat if possible)
    4. 1 tsp Italian seasoning
    5. 1 tsp salt
    6. ½ tsp pepper
- **Method**:
    1. Preheat oven to 400°F (200°C).
    2. In a bowl, mix turkey, egg white, breadcrumbs, and spices.
    3. Roll into golf-ball sized meatballs and place on a baking sheet.
    4. Bake for ~15–20 minutes or until internal temp is 165°F (74°C).
- **Pro Tip**: Serve with the Basic Tomato Sauce with a Punch (Recipe #8) over whole-grain pasta or zucchini noodles.

15. **Carb-Smart Quinoa Base**

- **Why It Rocks**: Complex carbs that pack a protein punch, too.
- **Ingredients** (makes ~4 cups cooked):
     1. 1 cup quinoa (rinsed)
     2. 2 cups vegetable or chicken stock (low-sodium if possible)
     3. Pinch of salt
- **Method**:
     1. Bring stock (and salt) to a boil in a medium saucepan.
     2. Stir in quinoa, reduce heat to low, cover.
     3. Cook ~15 minutes or until liquid is absorbed.
     4. Fluff with a fork.
- **Pro Tip**: Use this as the base for Buddha bowls, burrito fillings, or even breakfasts (mixed with eggs and veggies) for an all-day energy boost.

CHAPTER 3: MACRO MAYHEM—PROTEIN, CARBS, AND FATS—SORTED

A straight-talk breakdown on macros, plus a handful of foundational recipes you can customize for any meal.

Look, if you're serious about building muscle and cranking out high-powered workouts, you can't just wing it on the food front. In this chapter, we're blowing the lid off the **macro** mystery, cutting out all the BS, and giving you the straight facts on **protein, carbs, and fats**—plus a handful of go-to recipes you can tweak to fit your own macros like a glove.

Why Macros Matter (And Why You Should Care)

Think of **protein** as the bricks for your muscle "construction site." If you skimp on these, don't cry when your gains look more like a backyard shed than a skyscraper. **Carbs** get demonized all the time, but guess what? They're your body's **preferred energy source**. Use them wisely— swap out junky carbs for complex ones like oats, quinoa, or whole-grain pasta—and you'll find your tank stays fueled longer, so you can **smash** your next set or sprint. Finally, **fats**. Yeah, you need them. A zero-fat diet is a fast track to tanking your hormones and stalling your progress. Pick **healthy fats** like avocado, nuts, seeds, or even a drizzle of olive oil, and watch your body (and your mood) thank you.

Customizable Recipes for Real People

Here's the good news: once you wrap your head around the basics, you can **build meals** that actually work for you—your schedule, your tastes, and your macro targets. We'll lay out a few foundational recipes that are simple to swap around. Not feeling chicken? Try tofu or lean beef. Don't want white rice? Go with cauliflower rice or sweet potatoes. The point is to make your macros **malleable**, so you're not stuck choking down the same old bland chicken-and-broccoli combo every day.

So, if you're ready to **stop guessing** and start hitting your macro targets like a sniper, buckle up. We're about to break down each macro, show you how they fuel your progress, and then hook you up with flexible, flavor-packed recipes that prove healthy eating doesn't have to suck. Let's dive in and **demolish** any excuses standing between you and the gains you've been chasing.

Recipes Included: 10–15 macro-balanced base dishes (e.g., quick protein bowls or carb-smart)

1. Power Bowl Base

Why It Rocks

It's a **plug-and-play** bowl that crushes hunger and hits your macros without forcing you to choke down the same bland meal every day. Perfect if you want something simple yet packed with protein, carbs, and fats.

Ingredients (Serves 2)

- **Protein**: 1 lb lean ground turkey or chicken (or 1 block extra-firm tofu), seasoned as you like
- **Carbs**: 2 cups cooked brown rice or quinoa
- **Fats**: 1 ripe avocado (or 2 tbsp olive oil if you're not an avocado fan)
- **Veggies** (pick your favorites): spinach, cucumbers, cherry tomatoes, roasted peppers, etc.
- **Flavor Boost**: taco seasoning, chili powder, or your favorite spice mix

Method

1. **Cook your protein**: Brown turkey/chicken in a skillet with a splash of olive oil and your chosen seasonings. If using tofu, press it first, cube it, then sauté until golden.
2. **Prep your carbs**: Cook brown rice or quinoa according to package directions (usually 1 part grain to 2 parts water).
3. **Assemble**: In a bowl, layer the cooked rice/quinoa, then protein, then veggies. Top with avocado chunks (or drizzle olive oil).
4. **Season**: Finish with an extra sprinkle of chili powder or a dash of hot sauce if you like living on the edge.

Pro Tip

Cook **double** the protein and carbs at once, store them in airtight containers, and you've got instant lunch or dinner for days. Your future self will thank you for the hassle-free meal prep.

2. Mediterranean Chicken Wrap

Why It Rocks

Light, fresh, and bursting with flavor—this wrap keeps you **full** without feeling weighed down. Plus, you can swap the chicken for chickpeas or tofu if you're keeping it meat-free.

Ingredients (Makes 2 wraps)

- **Protein**: 2 grilled chicken breasts (or 1½ cups cooked chickpeas for a veg version)
- **Carbs**: 2 whole-wheat tortillas (or a wrap of your choice)
- **Fats**: 2–4 tbsp hummus (depending on how creamy you like it)
- **Veggies**: diced cucumbers, tomatoes, onions; toss in olives if you're feeling fancy
- **Flavor Boost**: a squeeze of lemon, sprinkle of oregano, salt, and pepper

Method

1. **Warm your wrap**: Heat each tortilla in a skillet for a few seconds—makes it easier to roll.
2. **Load up**: Spread hummus on the tortilla, layer sliced chicken (or chickpeas), then top with veggies.
3. **Season**: Squeeze lemon over the veggies, then sprinkle oregano, salt, and pepper.
4. **Wrap & Roll**: Fold in the sides and roll it up tightly so you don't end up wearing your lunch.

Pro Tip

Grill or bake multiple chicken breasts at once. These wraps are **perfect** for quick lunches—just grab, go, and crush your midday hunger without trashing your macros.

3. Veggie-Loaded Omelet

Why It Rocks

Starting your day with **protein and veggies** sets you up to dominate from the get-go. It's easy to customize—egg whites for lean protein, whole eggs for added fats, or a mix of both.

Ingredients (Serves 1)

- **Protein**: 3 egg whites + 1 whole egg (or 2 whole eggs if you need more fats)
- **Carbs**: Optional slice of whole-grain toast if you want extra fuel
- **Fats**: The egg yolk plus a sprinkle of cheese (if your macros allow)
- **Veggies**: chopped spinach, peppers, onions, tomatoes
- **Flavor Boost**: salt, pepper, hot sauce for the brave

Method

1. **Prep the veggies**: Sauté chopped onions and peppers in a non-stick pan until slightly soft. Add spinach and tomatoes last, so they don't get mushy.
2. **Add the eggs**: Whisk your egg whites and whole egg in a bowl; season with salt and pepper. Pour into the pan over the veggies.
3. **Cook it up**: Let the bottom set before folding or flipping. Cook until the eggs are firm but not dry—nobody wants a rubber omelet.
4. **Plate it**: Slide it onto a plate, add a hit of hot sauce if you're daring.

Pro Tip

Double or triple this recipe, store the omelets in meal-prep containers, and reheat throughout the week. That's how you stay **on track** without daily fuss.

4. High-Protein Stir-Fry

Why It Rocks

One pan, minimal cleanup, **loads of nutrients**. And it's the perfect excuse to clear out whatever veggies are about to die in your fridge.

Ingredients (Serves 3–4)

- **Protein**: 1 lb chicken breast, shrimp, or firm tofu (cubed)
- **Carbs**: 3 cups cooked brown rice or soba noodles
- **Fats**: 1 tbsp sesame oil (or a neutral oil if you prefer)
- **Veggies**: broccoli florets, bell peppers, onions, carrots—go wild
- **Flavor Boost**: soy sauce (low-sodium if you're not trying to bloat up), minced garlic, grated ginger, chili flakes

Method

1. **Heat oil** in a wok or large skillet over medium-high heat.
2. **Cook protein**: Add chicken/shrimp/tofu and sauté until browned/cooked through. Remove and set aside.
3. **Veggie time**: Stir-fry the veggies until crisp-tender—nobody wants limp broccoli.
4. **Combine**: Throw the protein back in, add soy sauce, garlic, ginger, and chili flakes. Stir to coat.
5. **Serve**: Plate over brown rice or noodles.

Pro Tip

Want to slash carbs? Swap the rice/noodles for cauliflower rice or just load up on more veggies. The sauce still packs a punch, so you won't miss the extra starch.

5. Simple Sheet-Pan Dinner

Why It Rocks

Everything goes on **one tray**, bakes together, and you're free to do your thing while dinner handles itself. Low effort, high reward.

Ingredients (Serves 2–3)

- **Protein**: 1 lb salmon fillet or chicken breasts
- **Carbs**: 2 sweet potatoes, sliced into wedges
- **Fats**: 2 tbsp olive oil (split between protein and potatoes)
- **Veggies**: broccoli florets, zucchini slices, bell peppers—your call
- **Flavor Boost**: garlic powder, paprika, salt, pepper

Method

1. **Preheat** oven to 400°F (200°C).
2. **Season potatoes**: Toss them with 1 tbsp oil, plus garlic powder, paprika, salt, pepper. Lay on half of a sheet pan.
3. **Season protein**: Use the other tbsp oil and more spices on the salmon or chicken. Place next to the potatoes.
4. **Add veggies**: Throw the veggies on the tray during the last 10–15 minutes so they don't turn to mush.
5. **Bake** for 20–25 minutes or until protein is cooked through.

Pro Tip

Double up on ingredients to meal-prep for the week. Sheet-pan dinners **reheat** like a charm, so your lazy future self will love you.

6. Lean Greek Yogurt Chicken Salad

Why It Rocks

Classic chicken salad flavor—without the mayo bomb that wrecks your macros. Greek yogurt ups the protein and keeps it creamy.

Ingredients (Serves 3–4)

- **Protein**: 3 cups cooked chicken breast (diced or shredded)
- **Carbs**: Serve in a whole-grain wrap, on top of rye bread, or over lettuce
- **Fats**: ½ cup plain Greek yogurt (instead of mayo)
- **Extras**: diced celery, red onion, grapes or dried cranberries (optional)
- **Flavor Boost**: salt, pepper, lemon juice

Method

1. **Mix it up**: In a large bowl, combine shredded chicken, Greek yogurt, celery, onions, and any optional add-ins.
2. **Season** with salt, pepper, and a splash of lemon juice.
3. **Chill it** in the fridge for at least 15–20 minutes to let flavors meld.

Pro Tip

Make a **large batch** and portion it out for quick lunches. Use different add-ins each time (like apples or walnuts) to keep it interesting while still hitting your macros.

7. Tofu & Veggie Foil Packets

Why It Rocks

Foil packets = **zero cleanup** and a foolproof way to keep tofu from turning into a soggy mess. Plus, you can easily portion out your carbs on the side.

Ingredients (Serves 2)

- **Protein**: 1 block firm tofu, drained and cubed
- **Carbs**: 1 cup cooked brown rice or quinoa (served on the side)
- **Fats**: 1 tbsp olive oil
- **Veggies**: cherry tomatoes, zucchini slices, onion chunks, bell peppers
- **Flavor Boost**: garlic powder, Italian seasoning, salt, pepper

Method

1. **Preheat** oven to 400°F (200°C).
2. **Assemble packets**: Lay out a large sheet of foil. Add cubed tofu and veggies, drizzle with olive oil, and sprinkle on seasonings.
3. **Seal it**: Fold the foil into a packet (make sure edges are tight so steam doesn't escape).
4. **Bake** for ~20 minutes, until tofu is slightly golden and veggies are cooked but not mushy.

Pro Tip

Make several packets at once—different proteins in each if you want variety. When they're done, **toss the foil** and call it a day.

8. Egg White Breakfast Burrito

Why It Rocks

A grab-and-go **protein powerhouse** that crushes morning hunger and keeps you from inhaling donuts at the office.

Ingredients (Serves 1)

- **Protein**: 4 egg whites (or 2 egg whites + 1 whole egg if you want some fats)
- **Carbs**: 1 whole-wheat tortilla
- **Fats**: optional sprinkle of cheese or a spoonful of avocado
- **Veggies**: diced onions, peppers, spinach
- **Flavor Boost**: salsa, hot sauce, cumin, salt, pepper

Method

1. **Cook the filling**: Whisk egg whites with a pinch of salt, pepper, and cumin. Sauté onions and peppers in a non-stick pan, then add eggs.
2. **Scramble**: Cook until eggs are firm but not dry.
3. **Assemble**: Warm the tortilla, lay down the egg mixture, top with cheese or avocado if you're feeling it, then drizzle salsa or hot sauce.
4. **Roll**: Fold in the sides and roll tight—don't let those gains spill out.

Pro Tip

Wrap it in foil and toss it in your bag. By the time you get to work or the gym, it'll still be warm enough to devour.

9. Turkey & Quinoa Stuffed Peppers

Why It Rocks

This is a **meal-prep MVP** that looks fancy but couldn't be easier. Plus, the bell pepper shell sneaks in extra veggies.

Ingredients (Serves 2–3)

- **Protein**: ½ lb lean ground turkey
- **Carbs**: 1 cup cooked quinoa
- **Fats**: 1 tbsp olive oil (for sautéing the turkey)
- **Peppers**: 3 large bell peppers (tops cut off, seeds removed)
- **Flavor Boost**: salt, pepper, garlic, onion, a dash of Italian seasoning

Method

1. **Preheat** oven to 375°F (190°C).
2. **Cook turkey**: Sauté ground turkey in olive oil with chopped onions/garlic until browned. Add seasonings.
3. **Mix in quinoa**: Stir cooked quinoa into the turkey mixture.
4. **Stuff & Bake**: Spoon the mixture into the hollowed peppers, stand them upright in a baking dish, and bake ~20 minutes or until peppers soften and turkey is fully cooked.

Pro Tip

Top with a little cheese or Greek yogurt if your macros allow. These babies reheat like a dream—pop them in the microwave at work and make your coworkers jealous.

10. Lazy One-Pot Protein Pasta

Why It Rocks

Everything goes into **one pot**—no separate boiling, no multiple pans. Perfect for those nights when you'd rather do anything else than scrub dishes.

Ingredients (Serves 3–4)

- **Protein**: 1 lb lean ground beef, turkey, or chicken sausage
- **Carbs**: 8–10 oz whole-wheat pasta (penne, rotini, or whatever)
- **Fats**: 1 tbsp olive oil for sautéing the protein
- **Sauce**: 1 can (14–15 oz) crushed tomatoes or tomato sauce
- **Extras**: 2–3 cups broth (chicken or veggie), diced onions, garlic, Italian seasoning

Method

1. **Sauté protein**: In a large pot, heat olive oil. Add ground meat or sausage, plus onions and garlic. Cook until browned. Drain extra fat if needed.
2. **Add liquids & pasta**: Stir in crushed tomatoes, broth, and pasta. Bring to a simmer.
3. **Simmer & Stir**: Keep an eye on it, stirring occasionally so the pasta doesn't stick. Cook until pasta is al dente—10–12 minutes usually.
4. **Season**: Toss in Italian seasoning, salt, pepper, or a pinch of chili flakes if you want some heat.

Pro Tip

Toss in a couple handfuls of spinach or kale at the end for extra micronutrients. Because a little green never killed anyone—unless you hate gains.

11. Protein-Packed Cauli Rice Skillet

Why It Rocks

Craving a grain-free twist without losing out on flavor or macros? **Cauliflower rice** is the perfect canvas for your protein of choice, plus any veggies you've got lying around.

Ingredients (Serves 2–3)

- **Protein**: 1 lb ground turkey or chicken (or ~12 oz tofu crumbles)
- **Carbs**: Cauliflower "rice" (about 3 cups)
- **Fats**: 1 tbsp olive oil for sautéing
- **Veggies**: Mushrooms, onions, bell peppers
- **Flavor Boost**: Soy sauce (low-sodium), garlic, black pepper, chili flakes

Method

1. **Heat oil** in a large skillet over medium-high heat.
2. **Cook protein**: Brown the turkey/chicken/tofu until cooked through. Drain extra liquid if needed.
3. **Add veggies**: Toss in mushrooms, onions, peppers; sauté until tender.
4. **Stir in cauli rice**: Mix in the cauliflower rice and season with soy sauce, garlic, black pepper, and chili flakes. Cook until cauliflower is slightly softened (about 5 minutes).

Pro Tip

Cauli rice cooks fast—keep an eye on it so it doesn't turn to mush. Finish with a drizzle of sesame oil if you want a richer flavor punch.

12. Spicy Tuna & Sweet Potato Cakes

Why It Rocks

Packed with protein and slow-digesting carbs, these cakes **satisfy cravings** while fueling your muscles. They're easy to meal-prep and even easier to heat up for a quick lunch or post-gym bite.

Ingredients (Makes 6–8 cakes)

- **Protein**: 2 cans tuna in water (5–6 oz each), drained
- **Carbs**: 1 large sweet potato, boiled and mashed (~1 cup)
- **Fats**: 1 egg (helps bind; plus healthy fats in the yolk)
- **Flavor Boost**: minced garlic, chopped green onion, chili powder or cayenne, salt, pepper
- **Extras**: ¼ cup whole-wheat breadcrumbs (optional, for texture)

Method

1. **Mash & Mix**: In a bowl, combine drained tuna, mashed sweet potato, egg, and seasonings. If it's too wet, add breadcrumbs.
2. **Form patties**: Shape into small cakes, about the size of your palm.
3. **Cook**: Sear in a lightly oiled skillet over medium heat for 3–4 minutes per side, until golden and heated through.

Pro Tip

Double the recipe and freeze half—these cakes **reheat** perfectly in a toaster oven or air fryer for a quick protein boost whenever you need it.

13. Muscle-Building Lentil Curry

Why It Rocks

Lentils are a **plant-based protein superstar**, and this curry delivers big on flavor without dumping your macros down the drain. Plus, you can batch-cook it for the whole week.

Ingredients (Serves 4–5)

- **Protein/Carbs**: 1½ cups dried lentils (rinsed)
- **Fats**: 1 tbsp coconut oil (or olive oil)
- **Veggies**: onion, garlic, diced tomatoes, spinach (or kale)
- **Flavor Boost**: curry powder, turmeric, cumin, salt, pepper
- **Liquid**: 4 cups vegetable broth (low-sodium if you're watching salt)

Method

1. **Sauté aromatics**: Heat oil in a large pot, add diced onion and garlic. Cook until fragrant.
2. **Season**: Sprinkle in curry powder, turmeric, cumin—toast the spices briefly to unlock flavors.
3. **Add lentils & broth**: Stir in lentils, pour in broth, bring to a simmer.
4. **Cook**: Cover and let it simmer ~20–25 minutes, or until lentils are tender. Stir in spinach/kale at the end.

Pro Tip

Need more protein? Stir in cooked chicken or shrimp at the end, or serve with a side of Greek yogurt for a cooling, protein-rich topping.

14. High-Energy Pork Tenderloin & Veggie Roast

Why It Rocks

Pork tenderloin is **lean, tender**, and protein-dense. Roast it alongside root veggies for a one-pan wonder that **powers** your workouts without trashing your macros.

Ingredients (Serves 3–4)

- **Protein**: 1 lb pork tenderloin, trimmed
- **Carbs**: 2 cups chopped root veggies (carrots, parsnips, or potatoes)
- **Fats**: 1–2 tbsp olive oil
- **Flavor Boost**: rosemary, thyme, garlic, salt, pepper
- **Extras**: optional drizzle of balsamic vinegar

Method

1. **Preheat** oven to 400°F (200°C).
2. **Season pork**: Rub tenderloin with olive oil, rosemary, thyme, garlic, salt, pepper.
3. **Veggie prep**: Toss chopped root veggies with a bit of olive oil, salt, and pepper.
4. **Roast**: Place pork and veggies on a sheet pan. Roast about 20–25 minutes, or until the internal temp of the pork hits 145°F (63°C).
5. **Rest & Slice**: Let pork rest 5 minutes before slicing to keep it juicy.

Pro Tip

Add a light drizzle of balsamic vinegar or apple cider vinegar to the pork right before serving for a tangy sweet twist—just enough to keep those taste buds entertained.

15. Loaded Baked Potato & Beef Skillet

Why It Rocks

It's like a baked potato on **muscle-building steroids**. Lean ground beef, potatoes, and a dash of cheese if your macros allow—straight-up comfort food that fits your macro blueprint.

Ingredients (Serves 2–3)

- **Protein**: 1 lb lean ground beef (90% lean or better)
- **Carbs**: 2 medium russet potatoes, cubed
- **Fats**: 1 tbsp olive oil (for cooking) + optional cheese topping
- **Veggies**: chopped onions, bell peppers, spinach (tossed in at the end if you want extra greens)
- **Flavor Boost**: salt, pepper, chili powder, or your favorite seasoning blend

Method

1. **Cook the beef**: In a skillet over medium-high heat, brown ground beef with onions, peppers, salt, pepper, and chili powder. Drain any excess grease.
2. **Par-cook potatoes**: Microwave cubed potatoes in a covered dish for 3–4 minutes (or boil them slightly) to speed things up.
3. **Combine**: Toss the potatoes into the skillet with the beef. Sauté until potatoes are crisp and cooked through.
4. **Optional cheese**: Sprinkle a bit on top if your macros allow, then cover until melted.

Pro Tip

For a leaner approach, swap the russet potatoes for sweet potatoes, or even use part sweet and part russet for a **carb combo** that'll keep your energy levels locked in.

These 15 new meals are meant to be tweaked and tailored to your specific macro targets. Swap proteins, dial carbs up or down, and don't be afraid to punch up the seasoning—boring food is for quitters. With these additions, you've got even more ammo in your meal-prep arsenal to feed your gains, keep you energized, and crush cravings before they even start. Now get in the kitchen and run the show.

CHAPTER 4: RISE AND GRIND—BREAKFASTS BUILT FOR BEASTS

Mornings are prime time for gains. Forget bland oatmeal; these high-protein, low-cal breakfasts snap you awake and keep you rolling till lunch.

Ever wonder why you're dragging by 10 a.m. and feel like your workouts are stuck in neutral? Here's a reality check: **mornings are prime time for gains**, and if your breakfast game is weak—or worse, nonexistent—you're essentially hitting the gym on an empty tank. Let's fix that, pronto. Forget those sad bowls of bland oatmeal and miserable slices of toast that do nothing but spike your blood sugar and send you crashing. This chapter is all about **high-protein, low-cal** breakfast options that **snap you awake** and keep you rolling straight through lunch without the mid-morning crash.

Why Breakfast Matters More Than You Think

When you're asleep, your body's been fasting (duh). By morning, it's **hungry for nutrients** to rebuild muscle tissue, replenish energy stores, and get your brain firing on all cylinders. Skip or skimp on breakfast, and you're sabotaging the entire day before it even begins. The good news? You don't need to crank out elaborate recipes at 6 a.m. We'll hook you up with **quick, foolproof** breakfasts that feed your muscles, not your excuses.

High Protein, Low Calorie—No Compromises

Here's the thing: big protein doesn't have to mean big calories. Think **egg whites + one or two whole eggs**, protein-packed Greek yogurt parfaits, or oatmeal souped up with a scoop of whey and fresh fruit. The trick is striking the right balance so you're not choking down flavorless cardboard. Want to turn that plain omelet into a beast-level meal? Toss in some lean turkey or sautéed veggies, top with a little cheese or hot sauce, and you're good to go. Bored of eggs? Shake things up with protein pancakes, overnight oats, or a breakfast burrito that'll make fast-food joints cry.

No Time? No Problem

"So I don't have 20 minutes to cook in the morning!" Save it. **Meal prep** is your friend. Whip up a batch of egg muffins on Sunday or portion out a few days' worth of overnight oats. Then all you have to do is **grab and go**, avoiding the drive-thru (and a total meltdown of your macros). If you can manage to swipe through Instagram when you wake up, you can handle reheating a prepped omelet for 45 seconds in the microwave.

Fuel Up and Dominate

Bottom line: a protein-packed, well-rounded breakfast **sets the stage** for everything else you do—your workout, your focus at work, and your mood. Start strong, and you'll keep that momentum rolling all day. Keep half-assing your morning meal, and you'll keep wondering why your lifts are stalling or why you're ready for a nap before noon. This chapter shows you **exactly** how to fuel up for the fight each morning. Ready to crank it up? Good. Flip the page, and let's turn your breakfast from a limp routine into a **muscle-feeding, energy-boosting**, all-out assault on hunger. Get hungry—and stay hungry.

Recipes Included: 30 high-protein, low-cal breakfast monsters (overnight oats, egg-white burritos, power pancakes, etc.)

Below are **30** high-protein, low-cal breakfast ideas—each with a quick breakdown of **Why It Rocks**, **Ingredients**, **Method**, and a final **Pro Tip** to crank up the flavor and convenience. They're designed to energize your mornings, feed your muscles, and keep your taste buds happy without blowing your macros. Feel free to **tweak and swap** ingredients to fit your dietary needs or personal tastes.

1. Overnight Super-Oats

Why It Rocks

No morning fuss—prep before bed, wake up to a protein powerhouse that keeps you fueled and focused.

Ingredients (Serves 1)

- ½ cup old-fashioned oats
- ½ cup low-fat milk (or almond milk)
- ½ cup Greek yogurt (plain, nonfat)
- 1 scoop whey or casein protein powder (vanilla or unflavored)
- 1 tsp chia seeds (optional)
- Sweetener to taste (stevia, honey, or none)

Method

1. In a sealable jar, stir together oats, milk, yogurt, protein powder, and chia seeds.
2. Sweeten if desired.
3. Refrigerate overnight.

Pro Tip

Add fresh fruit or a tablespoon of nut butter in the morning for extra flavor and texture.

2. Egg-White & Spinach Muffins

Why It Rocks

Perfect for meal-prep—cook a batch and you've got portable, protein-packed mini-meals for the whole week.

Ingredients (Makes ~12 muffins)

- 2 cups liquid egg whites (or separate ~12 egg whites)
- 1 cup chopped spinach (fresh or frozen, thawed & drained)
- ½ cup diced bell peppers
- ½ cup diced onions
- Salt, pepper, chili flakes to taste

Method

1. Preheat oven to 350°F (175°C).
2. Spray a muffin tin with cooking spray.
3. Mix egg whites, spinach, peppers, and onions in a bowl, then season.
4. Fill each muffin cup ¾ full.
5. Bake ~15–20 minutes, until set.

Pro Tip

Toss in some low-fat cheese or turkey bacon bits for extra flavor and protein.

3. Peanut Butter Banana Power Pancakes

Why It Rocks

High in protein, sweet without being a sugar bomb, and a killer way to start your day if you're craving comfort food.

Ingredients (Serves 1–2)

- ½ cup oats (blended into flour)
- 1 scoop whey protein (vanilla)
- 1 ripe banana, mashed
- 1 tbsp natural peanut butter
- ½ cup egg whites (or 1 whole egg + egg whites to ~½ cup total)
- ¼ tsp baking powder

Method

1. Combine oat flour, protein powder, baking powder in a bowl.
2. Add mashed banana, peanut butter, and egg whites. Stir into a thick batter.
3. Cook on a preheated non-stick skillet, ~2 minutes each side.

Pro Tip

Top with a drizzle of sugar-free syrup or extra banana slices for an indulgent feel without the calorie explosion.

4. Turkey Bacon Breakfast Quesadillas

Why It Rocks

Crispy tortilla, melty cheese, and the smoky flavor of turkey bacon—this is your **fast-food fix** without the grease pit.

Ingredients (Makes 1 quesadilla)

- 2 slices turkey bacon, cooked & chopped
- 2 egg whites + 1 whole egg, beaten
- 1 whole-wheat tortilla
- 2 tbsp low-fat shredded cheese
- Salt, pepper, any seasoning you like

Method

1. Scramble egg mixture in a non-stick pan. Season as desired.
2. Lay tortilla flat, sprinkle cheese, top with turkey bacon and scrambled eggs.
3. Fold tortilla in half, cook in a skillet until cheese melts and tortilla crisps.

Pro Tip

Add onions, peppers, or spinach to the scramble for extra nutrients and volume.

5. Veggie-Stuffed Egg White Burrito

Why It Rocks

A quick, wrap-and-go breakfast burrito with high protein and enough veggies to keep you satisfied for hours.

Ingredients (Serves 1)

- 4 egg whites (or 2 egg whites + 1 whole egg)
- 1 whole-wheat tortilla
- ¼ cup diced bell peppers
- ¼ cup diced onions
- ¼ cup diced mushrooms
- Salt, pepper, cumin (optional)

Method

1. Sauté peppers, onions, mushrooms in a non-stick pan.
2. Add egg whites; scramble until set.
3. Season with salt, pepper, and cumin.
4. Spoon onto tortilla, fold it up burrito-style.

Pro Tip

Wrap it in foil for an easy grab-and-go breakfast—no excuses for hitting the drive-thru instead.

6. Protein French Toast

Why It Rocks

A sweet morning treat that won't crush your macros, thanks to egg whites and a dash of protein powder.

Ingredients (Serves 1–2)

- 2 slices whole-grain bread
- ½ cup egg whites
- 1 scoop vanilla protein powder
- ¼ cup low-fat milk (or almond milk)
- ½ tsp cinnamon

Method

1. In a shallow dish, whisk egg whites, protein powder, milk, and cinnamon.
2. Dip bread on both sides, let it soak briefly.
3. Cook on a non-stick skillet over medium heat until golden brown on each side.

Pro Tip

Top with fresh fruit or sugar-free syrup for extra sweetness without the sugar crash.

7. Quick Cottage Cheese Fruit Bowl

Why It Rocks

Creamy, tangy cottage cheese loaded with fresh fruit for a protein punch that tastes like a dessert.

Ingredients (Serves 1)

- 1 cup low-fat cottage cheese
- 1 cup mixed berries (strawberries, blueberries, raspberries)
- 1 tbsp chopped nuts (almonds or walnuts) (optional)
- Sweetener to taste (honey, stevia)

Method

1. Scoop cottage cheese into a bowl.
2. Top with berries, drizzle honey or sprinkle stevia if desired.
3. Toss on chopped nuts for crunch (optional).

Pro Tip

Swap out fruit based on what's in season or what macros you have left—pineapple, peaches, or mango all work great.

8. Power Avocado Toast

Why It Rocks

It's the classic avocado toast, but we're boosting protein to keep you satisfied and pumped for the day.

Ingredients (Serves 1)

- 1 slice whole-grain bread
- ½ ripe avocado, mashed
- 2 egg whites (scrambled, poached, or fried)
- Salt, pepper, chili flakes

Method

1. Toast bread to desired crispness.
2. Spread avocado, sprinkle with salt, pepper, and chili flakes.
3. Top with cooked egg whites (or 1 whole egg if you want the yolk).

Pro Tip

For extra protein, add a slice of turkey breast or smoked salmon. The healthy fats + high protein = unstoppable morning fuel.

9. Creamy Overnight Oats with Berries

Why It Rocks

Another overnight oat twist, but with an extra creamy factor from Greek yogurt—and a bright burst of berries.

Ingredients (Serves 1)

- ½ cup rolled oats
- ½ cup low-fat milk (or almond milk)
- ½ cup plain Greek yogurt
- ½ cup mixed berries
- Sweetener (optional)

Method

1. Mix oats, milk, yogurt in a jar. Stir well.
2. Add sweetener if desired. Top with berries.
3. Refrigerate overnight.

Pro Tip

Use frozen berries if fresh aren't available; they'll thaw in the fridge and infuse the oats with flavor.

10. Chicken & Egg White Hash

Why It Rocks

High-protein spin on a breakfast hash—egg whites, diced chicken, and veggies for a hearty, low-cal start.

Ingredients (Serves 2)

- 4 egg whites
- 1 cup cooked chicken breast, chopped
- 1 cup diced potatoes (boiled or microwaved to speed up)

- ½ cup diced onions, peppers
- Salt, pepper, garlic powder

Method

1. Sauté onions, peppers in a non-stick skillet.
2. Add precooked potatoes and chicken, stir until heated.
3. Pour in egg whites, season with salt, pepper, garlic powder.
4. Cook until egg whites are set.

Pro Tip

Top with a little hot sauce or low-sugar ketchup to kick it up a notch without adding a pile of calories.

11. Protein-Packed Breakfast Muffins

Why It Rocks

Think mini-omelets in muffin form, but with added protein powder to up the muscle-building game.

Ingredients (Makes ~8–10 muffins)

- 6 egg whites + 2 whole eggs
- ½ scoop unflavored whey or casein protein
- 1 cup chopped spinach, peppers, onions
- Salt, pepper, paprika

Method

1. Preheat oven to 350°F (175°C).
2. Whisk eggs with protein powder until blended.
3. Stir in veggies, salt, pepper, paprika.
4. Pour into a greased muffin tin and bake ~15–20 mins.

Pro Tip

Experiment with add-ins: turkey bacon bits, low-fat cheese, or diced mushrooms. Meal-prep them for a week of superfast breakfasts.

12. Blueberry Protein Waffles

Why It Rocks

Fluffy waffles that actually help build muscle—score. Blueberries bring antioxidants without a ton of sugar.

Ingredients (Makes 2–3 waffles)

- ½ cup whole-wheat flour
- 1 scoop vanilla protein powder
- ½ tsp baking powder
- 1 egg white + 1 whole egg
- ¾ cup low-fat milk (or almond milk)
- ½ cup blueberries (fresh or frozen)

Method

1. Preheat waffle iron.
2. Mix flour, protein powder, baking powder.
3. Add eggs and milk; stir until just combined. Gently fold in blueberries.
4. Cook in waffle iron until golden.

Pro Tip

Skip the sugary syrups—top with a spoonful of Greek yogurt or a sprinkle of cinnamon instead.

13. Greek Yogurt Breakfast Parfait

Why It Rocks

Layers of fruit, yogurt, and granola give a **dessert-like vibe** without wrecking your macro count.

Ingredients (Serves 1)

- 1 cup plain Greek yogurt
- 1 cup mixed berries
- ¼ cup high-protein granola (or homemade oats + nuts)
- Drizzle of honey or pinch of stevia (optional)

Method

1. In a tall glass or bowl, layer yogurt, berries, and granola.
2. Sweeten if needed.

3. Repeat layers until you fill the glass.

Pro Tip

Make it the night before and keep it chilled—just add granola in the morning so it stays crunchy.

14. Salmon & Egg Whites on Whole-Grain Toast

Why It Rocks

Lean protein from egg whites meets healthy omega-3 fats from salmon. Breakfast of champions, indeed.

Ingredients (Serves 1)

- 1 slice whole-grain bread
- 2–3 egg whites, scrambled
- 2 oz smoked salmon or cooked salmon fillet
- Salt, pepper, dill (optional)

Method

1. Toast bread.
2. Scramble egg whites, season with salt, pepper, dill.
3. Layer egg whites and salmon on toast.

Pro Tip

Add a thin spread of light cream cheese or Greek yogurt if you want a creamier texture.

15. Sweet Potato Breakfast Skillet

Why It Rocks

Complex carbs from sweet potatoes + lean protein = a filling, energy-packed start to your day.

Ingredients (Serves 2)

- 1 large sweet potato, cubed and partially cooked (microwave ~3–4 mins)
- 4 egg whites + 1 whole egg
- ½ cup diced onions and peppers
- Salt, pepper, paprika

Method

1. Sauté onions, peppers in a non-stick skillet.
2. Add sweet potato cubes; cook until slightly crispy.
3. Stir in eggs, scramble until done.

Pro Tip

Sprinkle on some low-fat cheese or fresh herbs at the end for added flavor without many extra calories.

16. Banana Almond Protein Smoothie

Why It Rocks

A liquid breakfast for those who can't stomach solid food early. Almond butter + banana = a killer taste combo.

Ingredients (Serves 1)

- 1 scoop whey protein (vanilla)
- 1 banana (frozen if possible)
- 1 tbsp almond butter
- 1 cup almond milk (unsweetened)
- A handful of ice (optional)

Method

1. Add everything to a blender.
2. Blend until smooth.
3. Adjust thickness with more milk or ice.

Pro Tip

Toss in a handful of spinach for extra nutrients—you won't even taste it.

17. Apple Cinnamon Protein Oatmeal

Why It Rocks

Warm, comforting oats with a sweet apple twist—like apple pie without the sugar coma.

Ingredients (Serves 1)

- ½ cup rolled oats
- 1 scoop vanilla or cinnamon protein powder
- 1 cup water or low-fat milk
- ½ apple, diced
- ½ tsp cinnamon, dash of salt

Method

1. Cook oats in water/milk on stovetop or microwave.
2. Stir in protein powder, diced apple, cinnamon, salt.
3. Heat until apples soften slightly.

Pro Tip

Add a splash more liquid if it gets too thick after the protein powder. Top with chopped nuts for extra crunch.

18. Egg & Avocado Breakfast Sandwich

Why It Rocks

A hearty sandwich that's heavy on protein and healthy fats, minus the junk you'd get from a fast-food drive-thru.

Ingredients (Serves 1)

- 1 whole-wheat English muffin or bun
- 1 egg + 2 egg whites, cooked to your liking
- ¼ avocado, mashed
- Slice of tomato, optional spinach leaves
- Salt, pepper, dash of hot sauce if you're feeling it

Method

1. Toast the English muffin.
2. Spread mashed avocado on one side.
3. Layer with egg, tomato, spinach.
4. Season with salt, pepper, and hot sauce.

Pro Tip

Wrap in foil and take it with you—beats the greasy breakfast sandwich that'd sabotage your macros.

19. Zucchini & Egg Scramble

Why It Rocks

Zucchini ups your veggie intake without adding many carbs or calories. Great for volume-eaters.

Ingredients (Serves 1–2)

- 2 whole eggs + 2 egg whites
- 1 small zucchini, grated or diced
- ¼ cup diced onion
- Salt, pepper, garlic powder

Method

1. Sauté onion until slightly translucent.
2. Add zucchini, cook a few minutes until softened.
3. Whisk eggs, pour in, scramble until set.

Pro Tip

Sprinkle on some shredded low-fat cheese if your macros allow, or top with salsa for an extra kick.

20. Maple Cinnamon Protein Muffins

Why It Rocks

Meal-prep friendly muffins that stay moist, thanks to Greek yogurt, and pack a protein punch.

Ingredients (Makes ~6 muffins)

- 1 cup whole-wheat flour
- 1 scoop vanilla protein powder
- ½ cup plain Greek yogurt
- ¼ cup maple syrup (adjust to taste)
- 1 egg + 1 egg white
- 1 tsp baking powder, 1 tsp cinnamon

Method

1. Preheat oven to 350°F (175°C).
2. Whisk wet ingredients: yogurt, syrup, eggs.
3. In another bowl, mix flour, protein powder, baking powder, cinnamon.
4. Combine wet and dry, stir gently.
5. Fill a greased muffin tin, bake ~15–18 minutes.

Pro Tip

Substitute honey or mashed banana for maple syrup if you want less sugar. Store in airtight containers for a quick breakfast all week.

21. Green Machine Breakfast Smoothie

Why It Rocks

A veggie-packed smoothie that still tastes sweet enough to satisfy. Quick to prep, easy to gulp down.

Ingredients (Serves 1)

- 1 scoop vanilla protein powder
- 1 cup spinach or kale
- ½ banana
- ½ cup pineapple chunks
- 1 cup water or almond milk

Method

1. Throw everything in a blender.
2. Blend until smooth.

Pro Tip

Use frozen fruits for a thicker, creamier texture—plus you skip adding ice.

22. Egg-White Fried Rice (Breakfast Style)

Why It Rocks

Who says fried rice is only for dinner? This breakfast twist swaps normal eggs for egg whites and loads up on veggies.

Ingredients (Serves 2)

- 2 cups cooked brown rice (leftover rice works best)
- 1 cup egg whites
- 1 cup mixed veggies (peas, carrots, onions)
- 1 tbsp low-sodium soy sauce
- 1 tsp sesame oil (optional for flavor)

Method

1. Heat a non-stick pan or wok. Add sesame oil (if using), then veggies.
2. Add brown rice, stir-fry for a couple minutes.
3. Push rice aside, pour egg whites in, scramble quickly.
4. Mix everything together, add soy sauce to taste.

Pro Tip

Top with chopped green onions or a sprinkle of sriracha for a spicy kick that'll wake you right up.

23. Protein Banana Bread

Why It Rocks

Warm, cozy, and free from the sugar overload typical banana breads carry. Great for meal-prep.

Ingredients (Makes 1 loaf)

- 3 ripe bananas, mashed
- 1 scoop vanilla or unflavored protein powder
- 1½ cups whole-wheat flour
- 2 eggs (or 1 egg + 2 egg whites)
- 1 tsp baking soda
- ¼ cup honey or stevia to taste

Method

1. Preheat oven to 350°F (175°C).

2. In one bowl, combine mashed bananas, eggs, honey.
3. In another, mix flour, protein powder, baking soda.
4. Combine wet and dry, don't overmix.
5. Pour into a greased loaf pan, bake ~25–30 mins until a toothpick comes out clean.

Pro Tip

Add chopped nuts or dark chocolate chips if your macros allow. This bread also freezes well—slice and store for future cravings.

24. Power Yogurt Toast

Why It Rocks

Combine Greek yogurt and whole-grain toast for a protein-upgraded spin on a quick breakfast staple.

Ingredients (Serves 1)

- 1 slice whole-grain bread
- ¼ cup plain Greek yogurt
- 1 tsp honey (optional)
- Fruit toppings: sliced strawberries, blueberries, or banana

Method

1. Toast bread.
2. Mix Greek yogurt with honey if desired.
3. Spread yogurt on toast, top with fruit slices.

Pro Tip

Sprinkle a pinch of granola or chia seeds on top for added texture and micronutrients.

25. Scrambled Egg Whites with Chicken Sausage

Why It Rocks

Hearty protein from both eggs and lean chicken sausage, plus room to add veggies if you're feeling adventurous.

Ingredients (Serves 1–2)

- 1 or 2 chicken sausage links (look for reduced-fat)
- 4 egg whites
- ½ cup diced veggies (peppers, onions, etc.)
- Salt, pepper to taste

Method

1. Slice chicken sausage, sauté in a non-stick skillet.
2. Add diced veggies, cook until tender.
3. Pour in egg whites, scramble. Season.

Pro Tip

Serve with a slice of whole-grain bread or a small sweet potato for extra carbs if you need them for your morning workout.

26. Apple Pie Protein Smoothie

Why It Rocks

All the flavors of apple pie without the crust or sugar overload. Perfect if you crave something sweet in the a.m.

Ingredients (Serves 1)

- 1 scoop vanilla protein powder
- 1 small apple, chopped (freeze it for extra chill)
- ½ tsp cinnamon
- 1 cup almond milk (unsweetened)
- Handful of ice

Method

1. Blend apple, protein powder, cinnamon, and milk.
2. Add ice for thickness.
3. Blend until smooth.

Pro Tip

A pinch of nutmeg or cloves takes the "apple pie" flavor up a notch.

27. Protein-Infused Chia Pudding

Why It Rocks
A fiber bomb from chia seeds, plus an extra protein boost from yogurt or protein powder. Prep it at night, devour in the morning.

Ingredients (Serves 1)

- 1 tbsp chia seeds
- ½ cup almond milk (or low-fat milk)
- ½ scoop vanilla protein powder or ¼ cup Greek yogurt
- Sweetener to taste

Method

1. Stir all ingredients in a jar or bowl.
2. Let sit in fridge at least 2 hours, preferably overnight.
3. Add fruit or nuts in the morning for texture.

Pro Tip
If it's too thick in the morning, stir in a splash more milk. Easy fix.

28. Cinnamon Raisin Egg White Oatmeal

Why It Rocks
Combines the protein from egg whites with the cozy factor of cinnamon-raisin oats—like a bowl of nostalgia that fuels your day.

Ingredients (Serves 1)

- ½ cup oats
- 1 cup water (or milk)
- 2 egg whites
- 1 tbsp raisins
- ½ tsp cinnamon, pinch of salt

Method

1. Cook oats in water/milk.
2. Once it's hot, stir in egg whites slowly. Keep stirring to avoid clumps.
3. Add raisins, cinnamon, and salt. Simmer a bit longer until creamy.

Pro Tip

For extra sweetness, add a drizzle of sugar-free syrup or honey.

29. Broccoli & Cheese Egg Bake

Why It Rocks

Baked egg casseroles feed a crowd or just you for multiple mornings. Broccoli sneaks in nutrients, cheese adds flavor.

Ingredients (Makes ~6 squares)

- 6 eggs + 4 egg whites
- 1 cup chopped broccoli (lightly steamed)
- ½ cup low-fat shredded cheese
- Salt, pepper, garlic powder

Method

1. Preheat oven to 350°F (175°C).
2. Lightly steam or microwave broccoli so it's partially cooked.
3. Whisk eggs, egg whites, seasonings, fold in broccoli and cheese.
4. Pour into a greased baking dish, bake ~20–25 mins.

Pro Tip

Slice into squares once cooled. Grab one each morning and zap it in the microwave—instant breakfast, no fuss.

30. Savory Oatmeal with Turkey Bacon

Why It Rocks

Oatmeal doesn't have to be sweet. A savory spin with turkey bacon, egg whites, and veggies hits your macros from every angle.

Ingredients (Serves 1)

- ½ cup oats
- 1 cup water or low-sodium broth
- 2 egg whites (optional, stir in near the end)
- 2 slices turkey bacon, cooked & crumbled
- Diced veggies like tomatoes, spinach, or onions

Method

1. Cook oats in water/broth.
2. Stir in egg whites in the last minute or two if you want extra protein.
3. Top with turkey bacon and veggies.

Pro Tip

Season with salt, pepper, maybe even a dash of hot sauce. Don't knock savory oatmeal until you try it!

Bottom Line

With these **30 breakfast monsters**, you've got an army of **high-protein, low-cal** options ready to obliterate any excuses. Whether you crave sweet, savory, or quick smoothies, each of these recipes fuels your morning grind without gutting your macros. **Pick a favorite**, prep in bulk if you're time-crunched, and watch your energy and gains skyrocket before lunchtime even rolls around. Let's **rise and grind**, baby!

CHAPTER 5: MIDDAY MUSCLE—LUNCHES THAT CRUSH HUNGER

Enough with the sad desk salads. These lunches are packed with flavor and fueled by protein, so you can hit the gym—or the office—at full throttle.

Let's get something straight: if your idea of "lunch" is a limp piece of lettuce and a drizzle of sad dressing, your energy levels (and your gains) are taking a nosedive by mid-afternoon. **Enough with the sad desk salads** that leave you hungry twenty minutes later. Midday is prime time to refuel, recover, and ramp up for whatever the rest of your day demands—gym session, office grind, or chasing down a personal best. The lunches in this chapter are all about **maximizing flavor and protein** so you can stay on your A-game, crush your workouts, and skip the 3 p.m. crash.

Why Lunch Matters More Than You Think

By noon, your breakfast has done its job (assuming you had one worth mentioning), and your body is screaming for more nutrients. You've been busting your butt all morning—hustling at work, powering through errands, or maybe squeezing in an early workout. **Deprive your system now**, and you'll be dragging for the rest of the day. On the flip side, load up on the wrong kind of lunch— say, a greasy, carb-heavy takeout special—and you'll be wrestling with a **food coma** that kills your productivity. That's why every recipe in this chapter locks in **lean protein**, **smart carbs**, and just enough healthy fats to keep your brain and muscles firing on all cylinders.

Fuel for Performance and Focus

Don't think of lunch as a boring midday checkpoint. Think of it as **strategic refueling**. The right combination of macros can be the difference between owning your next gym session and phoning it in. Working a desk job? A lunch that's high in protein, moderate in carbs, and not drowning in fat keeps you alert, focused, and less likely to snack mindlessly come afternoon. Consider lunch your **launchpad**—your chance to recover from the morning's workload and prime your body for whatever's next.

Say Goodbye to Flavorless Meal Prep

"Meal prep" doesn't have to mean bland chicken and broccoli, day in and day out. If you're choking down the same dull plate of steamed veggies, it's no wonder you're tempted by the vending machine at 2 p.m. The lunches we're about to serve up are **bold, bursting with taste,** and designed to keep your macros in check without sacrificing an ounce of flavor. From build-your-own bowls to protein-packed wraps, you'll find plenty of reasons to actually **look forward** to lunchtime—and still feel confident you're fueling muscle growth, not packing on fluff.

Ready to Elevate Your Midday Game?

Grab your Tupperware, sharpen your appetite, and forget any excuse about not having time or not knowing what to cook. This chapter lays it all out: **no-BS recipes** that keep you satisfied while supercharging your gains. Whether you're headed back to the office, off to a mid-afternoon training session, or simply not in the mood for another sloppy takeout sandwich, these lunches have got you covered. Prepare to **dominate** your midday meal once and for all. Let's get to it.

Recipes Included: 25 knockout lunch options that bury boring meal plans (protein-packed wraps, bowls, salads that don't suck)

Below are **25 knockout lunch options** that bring the flavor **and** the gains, so you can ditch those sad, flavorless meal plans once and for all. Each recipe follows a similar format—**Why It Rocks**, **Ingredients**, **Method**, and a **Pro Tip**—so you can plug 'n' play into your lunchtime routine without skipping a beat. Let's bury boredom and fuel up for whatever the afternoon throws at you.

1. Beefed-Up Taco Salad

Why It Rocks
All the boldness of a taco, minus the mess. Lean ground beef, crisp veggies, and a homemade seasoning beat any limp takeout salad.

Ingredients (Serves 2)

- ½ lb lean ground beef (90% or better)
- 1 tbsp homemade taco seasoning (cumin, chili, garlic powder, etc.)
- 4 cups romaine or iceberg lettuce, chopped
- ½ cup diced tomatoes
- ½ cup black beans (optional)
- ¼ cup shredded low-fat cheese (or skip if you're cutting)
- Salsa or Greek yogurt as dressing

Method

1. Brown the beef in a non-stick skillet; add seasoning.
2. In a large bowl, layer lettuce, tomatoes, beans, cheese.
3. Top with seasoned beef.

4. Drizzle with salsa or Greek yogurt instead of calorie-bomb dressings.

Pro Tip
Want more crunch? Throw in a handful of baked tortilla strips or crushed baked chips—just keep an eye on the portion.

2. Spicy Sriracha Chicken Wrap

Why It Rocks
A protein-packed wrap that snaps you awake with a spicy kick—perfect for blasting through that midday slump.

Ingredients (Makes 1 wrap)

- 1 whole-wheat tortilla
- 1 chicken breast (5–6 oz), grilled and sliced
- 1 tbsp sriracha mixed with 1 tbsp Greek yogurt (for a creamy hot sauce)
- ¼ cup shredded lettuce
- ¼ cup diced tomatoes
- Salt, pepper

Method

1. Warm tortilla in a pan for a few seconds (makes it pliable).
2. Spread the sriracha-yogurt sauce.
3. Layer chicken, lettuce, tomatoes; season lightly.
4. Roll it up tight.

Pro Tip
Toss in extra veggies or even leftover roasted peppers to amp up nutrition and flavor without piling on extra calories.

3. Salmon & Avocado Power Bowl

Why It Rocks
Omega-3s from salmon meet creamy avocado on a bed of fiber-rich whole grains—fuel for your muscles and your brain.

Ingredients (Serves 2)

- 8 oz salmon fillet, cooked (baked, grilled, or pan-seared)

- 2 cups cooked brown rice or quinoa
- 1 ripe avocado, sliced
- 1 cup chopped cucumber, cherry tomatoes, or both
- Juice of ½ lemon, salt, pepper

Method

1. Cook salmon as you like (oven at 400°F for ~12–15 mins works great).
2. Assemble cooked rice/quinoa in a bowl.
3. Top with flaked or sliced salmon, cucumber, tomatoes, and avocado slices.
4. Drizzle lemon juice, salt, pepper.

Pro Tip
Make extra salmon the night before—then all you have to do is reheat and assemble at lunchtime.

4. Turkey & Pesto Lettuce Wraps

Why It Rocks
Cut the carbs a bit by ditching tortillas for lettuce leaves. The pesto brings flavor that'll make you forget about the bread.

Ingredients (Makes ~3–4 wraps)

- 8 oz turkey breast (sliced or shredded)
- 3–4 large romaine or iceberg lettuce leaves
- 2 tbsp pesto (store-bought or homemade)
- ½ cup diced tomatoes
- Salt, pepper

Method

1. Lay out lettuce leaves.
2. Spread a thin layer of pesto on each.
3. Layer turkey and tomatoes, season as needed.
4. Wrap it up, secure with toothpicks if they won't stay closed.

Pro Tip
Upgrade the crunch with some sliced cucumbers or onions if you've got time for more chop-chop.

5. Protein-Packed Taco Soup

Why It Rocks
Hearty, spicy, and easy to meal-prep. Load it with lean ground turkey and beans for a midday protein bomb.

Ingredients (Serves 3–4)

- 1 lb lean ground turkey
- 1 onion, diced
- 1 can diced tomatoes (14–15 oz)
- 1 can black beans, drained
- 1 packet (or homemade) taco seasoning
- 2 cups low-sodium chicken broth

Method

1. Brown turkey and onion in a large pot.
2. Stir in tomatoes, beans, seasoning, and broth.
3. Simmer ~15 minutes to let flavors meld.

Pro Tip
Serve with a dollop of Greek yogurt and a sprinkle of shredded cheese—or go extra-lean and skip the cheese altogether.

6. Chicken Caesar Wrap (Minus the Guilt)

Why It Rocks
All the Caesar flavor you love, but lightened up with Greek yogurt and lean chicken. Wrap it up and you're good to go.

Ingredients (Makes 1 wrap)

- 1 whole-wheat tortilla
- 1 chicken breast, grilled & sliced
- 2 cups romaine lettuce, chopped
- 2 tbsp Greek yogurt Caesar dressing (DIY: Greek yogurt + lemon + garlic + Parmesan)
- Salt, pepper

Method

1. Mix lettuce with dressing in a bowl.
2. Lay chicken slices down the center of the tortilla.

3. Top with dressed lettuce, roll up.

Pro Tip
Sprinkle a touch of Parmesan cheese if your macros allow, but go easy—it's strong stuff.

7. Asian-Inspired Shrimp & Veggie Stir-Fry

Why It Rocks
Quick, flavorful, and loaded with lean protein from shrimp. Great for batch-cooking—just reheat and devour.

Ingredients (Serves 2–3)

- 1 lb shrimp, peeled & deveined
- 2 cups mixed veggies (broccoli, bell peppers, carrots)
- 1 tbsp low-sodium soy sauce or tamari
- 1 tsp sesame oil (optional)
- 2 cups cooked brown rice

Method

1. Heat sesame oil in a wok or skillet.
2. Stir-fry veggies until slightly tender.
3. Add shrimp, cook until pink.
4. Splash in soy sauce, stir to coat.

Pro Tip
Bulk this up by tossing in extra tofu or chicken if you're looking to bump up protein even more.

8. Loaded Sweet Potato & Turkey Bowl

Why It Rocks
Sweet potatoes fuel your midday hustle, ground turkey fuels your gains, and together they bury bland lunches for good.

Ingredients (Serves 2)

- 2 medium sweet potatoes, baked or microwaved
- ½ lb lean ground turkey
- 1 tsp chili powder, salt, pepper
- 1 cup spinach or kale

- ¼ cup low-fat shredded cheese (optional)

Method

1. Brown turkey, season with chili powder, salt, pepper.
2. Microwave or bake sweet potatoes; split them open.
3. Stuff with turkey and spinach/kale.
4. Top with cheese if it fits your macros.

Pro Tip
Add a drizzle of hot sauce or Greek yogurt to bring it all together without adding loads of calories.

9. Greek Chickpea Salad

Why It Rocks
Plant-based protein from chickpeas, plus crisp veggies and tangy feta. Satisfying **and** refreshing.

Ingredients (Serves 2)

- 1 can chickpeas, drained and rinsed
- 1 cup diced cucumbers
- 1 cup diced tomatoes
- ¼ cup diced red onion
- ¼ cup crumbled feta (optional)
- Dressing: 1 tbsp olive oil + juice of ½ lemon + oregano + salt, pepper

Method

1. Combine chickpeas, veggies, and feta in a bowl.
2. Whisk dressing ingredients separately, pour over salad.
3. Toss well.

Pro Tip
Make it a heartier meal by adding grilled chicken or shrimp on top—still keeps it fresh, but ups the protein even more.

10. Tuna & Avocado Wrap

Why It Rocks
Creamy avocado replaces mayo for healthy fats, and tuna cranks up protein. Quick, simple, unstoppable.

Ingredients (Makes 1 wrap)

- 1 whole-wheat tortilla
- 1 can tuna in water, drained
- ½ avocado, mashed
- ¼ cup diced celery
- Salt, pepper, lemon juice

Method

1. Mash tuna with avocado, celery, and seasonings.
2. Spread onto tortilla.
3. Roll it up, slice in half, and demolish.

Pro Tip
Throw in some hot sauce or diced pickles for extra zip.

11. Turkey & Veggie Pita Pocket

Why It Rocks
Pitas are a great alternative to standard bread, and turkey with crunchy veggies is guaranteed to fill you up without feeling sluggish.

Ingredients (Makes 1 pocket)

- 1 whole-wheat pita
- 4–5 oz sliced turkey breast
- ¼ cup shredded carrots
- ¼ cup cucumbers, sliced
- 1 tbsp hummus

Method

1. Warm pita, cut open one side to make a pocket.
2. Spread hummus inside.
3. Stuff with turkey, carrots, cucumbers.

Pro Tip

Add a sprinkle of za'atar or paprika to the hummus for a subtle flavor boost that'll have you ditching store-bought sauces.

12. Quinoa Chicken Veggie Bowl

Why It Rocks

Quinoa brings both carbs and extra protein, while chicken seals the deal for a lunchtime muscle builder.

Ingredients (Serves 2)

- 1 cup quinoa (cooked)
- 1 chicken breast (8–10 oz), diced
- 1 cup mixed veggies (zucchini, peppers, onions)
- 1 tbsp olive oil
- Salt, pepper, Italian seasoning

Method

1. Sauté chicken in olive oil, season with salt, pepper, Italian herbs.
2. Add veggies, cook till tender.
3. Stir in cooked quinoa.
4. Adjust seasoning.

Pro Tip

Cook a big batch of quinoa early in the week, then just toss it in with whatever protein and veggies you have on hand.

13. Tofu & Brown Rice Buddha Bowl

Why It Rocks

A veggie-friendly lunch loaded with protein from tofu and a rainbow of nutrients from fresh veggies.

Ingredients (Serves 2)

- 1 block extra-firm tofu, pressed & cubed
- 2 cups cooked brown rice
- 1 cup roasted veggies (broccoli, carrots, bell peppers)
- 2 tbsp low-sodium soy sauce or teriyaki sauce

- 1 tsp sesame oil (optional)

Method

1. Bake or sauté tofu cubes until golden.
2. Arrange brown rice in a bowl, add roasted veggies and tofu.
3. Drizzle with soy/teriyaki sauce, add sesame oil if you want.

Pro Tip
Marinate the tofu beforehand in a mixture of soy sauce, garlic, and a dash of honey for extra flavor punch.

14. Southwest Chicken Salad Jar

Why It Rocks
Layer everything in a jar—easy to pack, easy to eat. Southwest flavors bring heat without the cheat.

Ingredients (Makes 1 jar)

- 1 cup cooked chicken breast, diced
- 1 cup chopped romaine
- ¼ cup black beans, rinsed
- ¼ cup corn (fresh or frozen, thawed)
- ¼ cup diced tomatoes
- Dressing: salsa + Greek yogurt, mixed

Method

1. In a tall jar, layer dressing at the bottom, then beans, corn, tomatoes, chicken, and top with lettuce.
2. Keep chilled until lunch.
3. Shake before eating or dump into a bowl.

Pro Tip
Add diced jalapeños or hot sauce if you want that authentic Southwest burn.

15. Lentil & Veggie Soup

Why It Rocks
Lentils deliver a hefty dose of protein and fiber, making this soup super filling without weighing you down.

Ingredients (Serves 3–4)

- 1 cup dried lentils, rinsed
- 1 onion, diced
- 1 carrot, sliced
- 2 stalks celery, chopped
- 4 cups low-sodium broth
- Salt, pepper, thyme

Method

1. Sauté onion, carrot, celery in a pot.
2. Add lentils and broth.
3. Simmer ~20–25 mins until lentils are tender. Season with salt, pepper, thyme.

Pro Tip
Make a big batch on Sunday. Soups taste even better the next day, and you can freeze portions for later.

16. Baked Cod & Sweet Potato Sheet Pan

Why It Rocks
Fish often gets ignored at lunch—bake cod with sweet potatoes on one sheet and power up with lean protein plus complex carbs.

Ingredients (Serves 2)

- 2 cod fillets (~5–6 oz each)
- 2 sweet potatoes, cubed
- 1 tbsp olive oil
- Salt, pepper, paprika

Method

1. Preheat oven to 400°F (200°C).
2. Toss sweet potatoes with olive oil, salt, pepper, paprika; spread on sheet.
3. Bake ~10 mins, then add cod fillets (seasoned with salt/pepper).

4. Bake another 10–12 mins until fish flakes and potatoes are tender.

Pro Tip
Add quick-cooking veggies (zucchini, bell peppers) in the last few minutes if you want an all-in-one meal.

17. Buffalo Chicken Lettuce Boats

Why It Rocks
Craving wings at noon? Buffalo chicken lettuce wraps let you indulge in that spicy tang without inhaling a bucket of fried skin.

Ingredients (Makes ~3 boats)

- 1 chicken breast, shredded
- 2 tbsp buffalo sauce (or hot sauce + melted light butter)
- 3 romaine leaves
- 1 tbsp Greek yogurt or low-fat ranch (optional)

Method

1. Toss shredded chicken in buffalo sauce.
2. Spoon into lettuce leaves.
3. Drizzle yogurt or ranch if you need to cut the heat.

Pro Tip
Prep extra chicken in buffalo sauce. Use it in wraps, salads, or top your next pizza if that's your jam.

18. Tuna Nicoise-Inspired Salad

Why It Rocks
A nod to the classic French salad—lighter but still loaded with protein from tuna and eggs, plus crisp veggies.

Ingredients (Serves 2)

- 1 can tuna in water, drained
- 2 hard-boiled eggs, quartered
- 2 cups mixed greens
- ½ cup cooked green beans (fresh or frozen)

- 1 small boiled potato, sliced
- Dressing: olive oil, lemon juice, Dijon mustard, salt, pepper

Method

1. Whisk dressing ingredients in a small bowl.
2. Arrange greens, tuna, eggs, green beans, and potato in a large bowl.
3. Drizzle dressing over top.

Pro Tip
Sub in sweet potato if you prefer. Keep it cold or pack the components separately to maintain freshness.

19. Baked Turkey Meatballs & Zoodles

Why It Rocks
Lean turkey meatballs + zucchini noodles for a low-carb lunch that still satisfies those Italian cravings.

Ingredients (Serves 2–3)

- 1 lb ground turkey
- ½ cup breadcrumbs (whole-wheat if possible)
- 1 egg
- 1 tsp Italian seasoning, salt, pepper
- 2 zucchinis, spiralized (zoodles)

Method

1. Preheat oven to 400°F (200°C).
2. Combine turkey, breadcrumbs, egg, and seasonings; form meatballs.
3. Bake on a sheet for ~15–20 mins or until cooked through.
4. Meanwhile, sauté zoodles quickly with salt, pepper.

Pro Tip
Top with a bit of marinara sauce or crushed tomatoes for real "spaghetti and meatballs" vibes—minus the carb overload.

20. Teriyaki Chicken & Veggie Bowl

Why It Rocks
Homemade teriyaki sauce (light on sugar) plus lean chicken and veggies = a sweet-savory lunch that dominates hunger.

Ingredients (Serves 2)

- 2 chicken breasts, cubed
- 2 cups mixed veggies (broccoli, carrots, onions)
- 2 cups cooked brown rice
- Homemade teriyaki: ¼ cup soy sauce, 1 tbsp honey, 1 tsp cornstarch, garlic, ginger

Method

1. Stir-fry chicken until browned; remove.
2. Stir-fry veggies.
3. Mix teriyaki ingredients in a small bowl, add to pan with chicken. Let thicken briefly.
4. Serve over rice.

Pro Tip
Adjust sweetness by tweaking the honey or using a sugar substitute if you're cutting down.

21. BBQ Pulled Chicken Sandwich

Why It Rocks
BBQ flavor doesn't have to mean a cheat meal. Use a light BBQ sauce and lean chicken for a sandwich that keeps you satisfied without guilt.

Ingredients (Makes 2 sandwiches)

- 2 chicken breasts, slow-cooked or pressure-cooked, then shredded
- ¼ cup low-sugar BBQ sauce
- 2 whole-wheat buns
- Coleslaw (optional, or use light coleslaw dressing)

Method

1. Mix shredded chicken with BBQ sauce in a pot over low heat.
2. Pile onto buns.
3. Add coleslaw or lettuce for crunch.

Pro Tip
Make a batch of shredded chicken on Sunday—use it all week in wraps, salads, or this killer sandwich.

22. Spicy Chickpea & Spinach Stew

Why It Rocks
Protein from chickpeas, iron from spinach, a spicy kick to keep it interesting—all in one easy pot.

Ingredients (Serves 3–4)

- 1 can chickpeas, drained
- 2 cups fresh spinach
- 1 onion, diced
- 1 can diced tomatoes (14–15 oz)
- 1 tsp chili powder, 1 tsp cumin, salt, pepper

Method

1. Sauté onion until translucent.
2. Add tomatoes, chickpeas, seasonings; simmer ~10 mins.
3. Stir in spinach until wilted.

Pro Tip
Pair it with a piece of whole-grain bread or pour it over brown rice if you need an extra carb boost.

23. Beef & Broccoli Rice Bowl

Why It Rocks
A leaner, homemade twist on the takeout classic. Control the sauce, ditch the MSG, and keep the flavor.

Ingredients (Serves 2)

- 8 oz lean steak (sirloin or flank), sliced
- 2 cups broccoli florets
- 2 cups cooked brown rice
- 1 tbsp low-sodium soy sauce, 1 tsp cornstarch, garlic, ginger

Method

1. Stir-fry beef in a hot skillet. Remove once browned.
2. Add broccoli, a splash of water, cook until tender-crisp.
3. Mix soy sauce, cornstarch, garlic, ginger; pour into pan with beef.
4. Serve over rice.

Pro Tip

Slice beef against the grain for tenderness. And if you crave more heat, toss in chili flakes or sriracha.

24. Mixed Bean & Chicken Burrito Bowl

Why It Rocks

A Chipotle-style bowl without the monstrous calorie count. Beans, chicken, veggies—simple, satisfying, macro-friendly.

Ingredients (Serves 2)

- 2 cups cooked brown rice
- 1 chicken breast, grilled & cubed
- 1 cup mixed beans (pinto, black, kidney)
- 1 cup diced bell peppers, onions
- Toppings: salsa, Greek yogurt, jalapeños

Method

1. Warm beans in a small pot, season with salt, pepper, chili powder.
2. Layer rice in a bowl, add beans, chicken, peppers, onions.
3. Top with salsa, Greek yogurt, jalapeños if you like it spicy.

Pro Tip

Make your own taco seasoning to avoid hidden sugars and insane sodium found in some store-bought packets.

25. Tomato & Mozzarella Stuffed Chicken

Why It Rocks

A high-protein dish that feels like gourmet without the fancy price tag or time suck. Mozzarella + tomato = unstoppable combo.

Ingredients (Serves 2)

- 2 chicken breasts
- 1 tomato, sliced thin
- 2–4 slices fresh mozzarella (light if possible)
- Basil, salt, pepper
- 1 tbsp olive oil

Method

1. Preheat oven to 375°F (190°C).
2. Slice a "pocket" into each chicken breast.
3. Stuff with tomato slices, mozzarella, and basil.
4. Season outside with salt, pepper; drizzle with olive oil.
5. Bake ~20–25 mins until chicken is fully cooked (internal temp 165°F/74°C).

Pro Tip
Serve with a side of roasted veggies or a small portion of whole-wheat pasta if you need more carbs. Drizzle a bit of balsamic glaze for next-level flavor.

Wrapping It Up

That's **25** midday monsters, each one designed to **bury boring lunches** and keep your muscles (and taste buds) fired up. Whether you're a wrap fiend, a bowl junkie, or a soup-and-salad type, there's something here to level up your lunch game. **Pick a couple**, prep them in bulk, and watch your **afternoons go from sluggish** to **dominating** in no time. Bon appétit, and remember: **midday** is the **new prime time** for gains if you do it right.

CHAPTER 6: NIGHTTIME KNOCKOUTS—DINNERS THAT DON'T MESS AROUND

No more watery soups or limp veggies. Get hearty, explosive-flavor meals that feed your muscles all night, so you wake up ready to conquer.

Listen up: dinner isn't just the last meal of the day; it's your **secret weapon** for overnight muscle building. If you're winding down with watery soups and sad, limp veggies, you're basically inviting your gains to tap out. Instead, it's time to finish strong with **hearty, explosive-flavor meals** that keep your metabolism fired up and your muscles primed while you sleep. So when your alarm goes off, you're not just **ready**, you're **running** to crush your next workout.

Why Dinner Is Non-Negotiable

You've been grinding all day—maybe you hit the gym, dominated at work, handled errands—and now your body is screaming for nutrients. Starve yourself at night, and guess what? Your muscles won't have the fuel they need to **recover** and **grow**. Overdo it on junk, and you'll wake up feeling like you got trampled by a herd of elephants. The fix? **Balanced dinners** that deliver protein (to feed muscles), complex carbs (to replenish glycogen and keep energy levels stable), and healthy fats (to help hormones and satiety). No extremes, no excuses—just a rock-solid meal to set you up for success.

Crush Late-Night Cravings

We've all been there: it's 9 p.m., and suddenly that bag of chips in the pantry starts whispering your name. Here's the deal: if you've eaten a satisfying, protein-heavy dinner packed with flavor, you won't be trolling your cabinets for garbage an hour later. Cravings usually strike when your meals are too small, too bland, or missing key nutrients. So let's **bury** that problem with dinners that actually fill you up—and yes, taste damn good.

Big on Flavor, Light on Regret

People hear "hearty dinner" and imagine a mountain of grease, cream sauces, or starchy sides that'll have you crawling to bed with a bloated gut. Forget that. The **Nighttime Knockouts** in this chapter prove you can have a **massive flavor payoff** without drowning in calories. We're talking lean proteins—think chicken, fish, turkey, even lean beef—paired with colorful veggies and bold seasonings that might just blow your taste buds off (in a good way). Add in some whole grains, sweet potatoes, or other smart carbs, and you've got a meal that'll keep your macros in check and your taste buds on cloud nine.

Wake Up Ready to Conquer

What happens overnight doesn't stay overnight—your recovery, muscle repair, and hormone regulation happen while you snooze. Set your body up with the right nutrients before you crash, and you'll **bounce out of bed** with more energy and less soreness. Bonus: you'll skip the sluggish morning "hangover" that follows a greasy, carb-loaded feast. After all, how you **end** your day often determines how you **start** the next one.

Lock In or Get Left Behind

So if you're still choking down flavorless dinners or ignoring that meal altogether, consider this your wake-up call. The recipes in this chapter don't mess around: they're designed to **give your muscles what they need**, knock out hunger, and keep you on track—even while you catch some Z's. Get ready to crank up the **taste factor** and supercharge your overnight gains. Tomorrow's battle begins tonight—time to eat like you mean it.

Recipes Included: 20 quick-fix snacks (protein bars, meatless bites, on-the-go shakes)

Below are 40 hearty dinner recipes built to light up your taste buds, feed your muscles, and keep your nights anything but boring. Each one delivers explosive flavor while staying smart about lean protein and balanced macros.

1. Creamy Tuscan Chicken (Without the Crazy Cream)

Why It Rocks
Classic Tuscan chicken flavor but lightened up so you can dig in guilt-free. Lean chicken in a garlicky, tomato-packed sauce that's way more satisfying than your usual bland protein bomb.

Ingredients (Serves 2–3)

- 1 lb chicken breast, cut into strips
- 1 tbsp olive oil
- 3 cloves garlic, minced
- 1 cup diced tomatoes (fresh or canned, drained)
- 1 cup baby spinach leaves
- ½ cup low-fat milk (or unsweetened almond milk)
- 1 tbsp cornstarch (mixed with 2 tbsp water)
- Salt, pepper, Italian herbs (basil, oregano)

Method

1. **Sear** chicken in a hot skillet with olive oil. Season with salt, pepper. Cook until browned on both sides; remove.
2. **Sauté** garlic in the same pan until fragrant. Add diced tomatoes, spinach, and Italian herbs.
3. **Pour** in milk; stir in cornstarch slurry to thicken. Simmer for 2–3 minutes.
4. **Return** chicken to the pan, spoon the sauce over it. Simmer another 2–3 minutes until fully cooked.

Pro Tip

Serve over whole-wheat pasta or with a side of roasted veggies for a complete, protein-heavy dinner that'll make your taste buds sing.

2. Lean Beef & Barley Stew

Why It Rocks

Big stew energy without the fat overload. Barley adds fiber and a satisfying chew, while lean beef gives you that protein punch to keep muscles primed.

Ingredients (Serves 4–5)

- 1 lb lean stewing beef (round or sirloin, trimmed)
- 1 tbsp olive oil
- 1 onion, chopped
- 2 carrots, sliced
- 2 celery stalks, sliced
- ½ cup pearl barley (rinsed)
- 4 cups low-sodium beef or vegetable broth
- Salt, pepper, thyme

Method

1. **Brown** beef in a large pot with olive oil. Season generously with salt, pepper.
2. **Add** onion, carrots, celery; cook until onions go translucent.
3. **Stir in** barley and broth. Add thyme.
4. **Simmer** ~30–40 minutes until barley is tender and beef is fork-tender.

Pro Tip

Stews taste even better the next day—so make extra and enjoy leftover gains.

3. Spicy Shrimp & Veggie Stir-Fry

Why It Rocks
Explosive heat from chili sauce or sriracha, plus plump shrimp loaded with lean protein. Minimal carbs if you want to keep it light—just add noodles or rice if you need more fuel.

Ingredients (Serves 2–3)

- 1 lb shrimp (peeled & deveined)
- 2 cups mixed veggies (zucchini, bell peppers, onions, broccoli)
- 1 tbsp olive or sesame oil
- 2 tbsp low-sodium soy sauce
- 1 tbsp sriracha or chili paste (adjust for heat)
- 2 cloves garlic, minced
- 1 tsp cornstarch mixed with 1 tbsp water (for thickening)

Method

1. **Heat** oil in a wok or skillet.
2. **Toss** in veggies, stir-fry until crisp-tender. Remove and set aside.
3. **Cook** shrimp with garlic, add soy sauce and sriracha. Stir in cornstarch slurry to thicken.
4. **Combine** with veggies, toss for a minute or so, and serve hot.

Pro Tip
If you're bulking or need extra carbs, serve over brown rice or whole-wheat noodles. If you're cutting, just scoop it into a bowl and chow down.

4. One-Pan Salmon & Veggies

Why It Rocks
Omega-3 rich salmon plus an array of roasted veggies in **one** pan. Easy cleanup, maximum taste—zero excuses.

Ingredients (Serves 2)

- 2 salmon fillets (~6 oz each)
- 1 cup broccoli florets
- 1 cup zucchini slices
- 1 tbsp olive oil
- Salt, pepper, lemon pepper seasoning (optional)

Method

1. **Preheat** oven to 400°F (200°C).
2. **Toss** veggies in olive oil, salt, pepper. Spread on one side of a foil-lined baking sheet.
3. **Season** salmon fillets and place on the other side of the sheet.
4. **Roast** ~12–15 minutes until salmon flakes and veggies are tender.

Pro Tip

Finish with a squeeze of lemon juice or a drizzle of low-cal balsamic glaze to give it that final pop.

5. Turkey Bolognese Over High-Protein Pasta

Why It Rocks

Classic Italian flavors minus the heavy ground beef. Turkey Bolognese is lighter, and high-protein pasta keeps your macros on track.

Ingredients (Serves 3–4)

- 1 lb ground turkey (93% lean or better)
- 1 onion, diced
- 1 carrot, grated (optional but adds sweetness)
- 2 cloves garlic, minced
- 1 can (14–15 oz) crushed tomatoes
- ½ tsp dried basil, ½ tsp dried oregano
- Salt, pepper
- 8–10 oz high-protein pasta (chickpea, lentil, or whole-wheat)

Method

1. **Sauté** turkey, onion, carrot, garlic in a deep pan until turkey is browned. Season with salt, pepper.
2. **Add** crushed tomatoes, basil, oregano. Simmer ~15 minutes.
3. **Cook** pasta separately, drain, then combine with sauce.

Pro Tip

Want more veggies? Toss in chopped zucchini or bell peppers for extra fiber and flavor.

6. Jamaican Jerk Chicken Thighs

Why It Rocks
Chicken thighs may have a bit more fat than breasts, but they explode with flavor—especially with a fiery jerk marinade. Perfect if you're looking for a bolder, juicier protein hit.

Ingredients (Serves 3–4)

- 1½ lb chicken thighs, boneless & skinless
- Jerk marinade: 1 tbsp jerk seasoning + 1 tbsp olive oil + juice of ½ lime
- Salt, pepper
- Optional sides: sweet potatoes, plantains, or a simple salad

Method

1. **Marinate** chicken thighs in jerk mixture for at least 30 minutes (overnight for best results).
2. **Preheat** oven to 400°F (200°C) or heat a grill.
3. **Cook** chicken ~20–25 minutes or until internal temp hits 165°F (74°C).

Pro Tip
Make a quick salsa with diced mango, lime juice, and cilantro to top off that spicy jerk flavor.

7. Lean Pork Tenderloin & Apples

Why It Rocks
Pork tenderloin is underrated—when cooked right, it's lean, tender, and packed with protein. Adding apples sweetens the deal without dumping sugar.

Ingredients (Serves 2–3)

- 1 lb pork tenderloin, trimmed
- 1 tbsp olive oil
- 1 apple, thinly sliced
- 1 onion, sliced
- Salt, pepper, thyme

Method

1. **Season** pork with salt, pepper, thyme.
2. **Sear** in an oven-safe skillet with olive oil.
3. **Add** apple, onion slices around the pork.
4. **Transfer** to 375°F (190°C) oven, roast ~20 minutes or until internal temp is 145°F (63°C).

Pro Tip

Let the meat rest a good 5 minutes before slicing—keeps all those tasty juices locked in.

8. Hearty Chicken & Sweet Potato Stew

Why It Rocks

Sweet potatoes bring a lower-glycemic carb to the table, while chicken keeps it lean. Perfect for a cozy, muscle-building dinner.

Ingredients (Serves 3–4)

- 1 lb chicken breast, cubed
- 1 onion, chopped
- 2 sweet potatoes, peeled & cubed
- 3 cups low-sodium chicken broth
- 1 tsp smoked paprika, salt, pepper

Method

1. **Sauté** chicken and onion in a large pot until lightly browned.
2. **Add** sweet potato cubes, broth, paprika.
3. **Simmer** ~15–20 minutes until potatoes are tender, season to taste.

Pro Tip

For extra greens, stir in spinach or kale at the end. Let it wilt for a nutrient boost that doesn't mess with flavor.

9. Turkey Meatball Zucchini Boats

Why It Rocks

Think "meatball sub," but replace the bread with zucchini. Extra lean, extra veg, zero flavor sacrificed.

Ingredients (Makes ~4 boats)

- 1 lb ground turkey
- 1 egg
- ¼ cup breadcrumbs (whole-wheat if possible)
- 2 zucchini, halved lengthwise & scooped
- 1 cup tomato sauce (low-sugar, low-sodium)
- Italian seasoning, salt, pepper

Method

1. **Preheat** oven to 375°F (190°C).
2. **Mix** turkey, egg, breadcrumbs, seasoning; form small meatballs.
3. **Arrange** zucchini halves on a baking sheet, spoon some tomato sauce inside.
4. **Place** meatballs on top, drizzle with more sauce.
5. **Bake** ~20–25 minutes until meatballs are cooked.

Pro Tip

Sprinkle a little low-fat mozzarella on top during the last 5 minutes for a melty finish.

10. High-Protein Veggie Chili

Why It Rocks

Beans, beans, and more beans—plus you can toss in ground turkey or keep it meat-free. Either way, the flavor is explosive, and the protein is legit.

Ingredients (Serves 4–5)

- 1 can black beans, 1 can kidney beans, drained
- 1 onion, diced
- 1 bell pepper, diced
- 1 can (14–15 oz) diced tomatoes
- 1 tbsp chili powder, 1 tsp cumin
- Optional: ½ lb ground turkey

Method

1. **Sauté** onion, pepper. If adding turkey, brown it here.
2. **Add** beans, tomatoes, chili powder, cumin.
3. **Simmer** ~20 minutes to let flavors intensify.

Pro Tip

Top with Greek yogurt, chopped green onions, or a sprinkle of cheese. For extra heat, toss in diced jalapeños.

11. Spaghetti Squash & Lean Meat Sauce

Why It Rocks

Spaghetti squash is a killer stand-in for pasta if you're cutting carbs. Top it with a lean beef or turkey sauce, and you've got a dinner that won't weigh you down.

Ingredients (Serves 2–3)

- 1 medium spaghetti squash
- ½ lb lean ground beef or turkey
- 1 small onion, diced
- 1 can (14–15 oz) crushed tomatoes
- Italian seasoning, salt, pepper

Method

1. **Roast** squash: Halve, remove seeds, season with salt. Bake at 400°F (200°C) ~30–40 mins.
2. **Brown** meat with onions; add tomatoes, seasoning. Simmer.
3. **Shred** cooked squash with a fork into "noodles."
4. **Top** squash strands with meat sauce.

Pro Tip

Don't skip seasoning the squash itself—drizzle a little olive oil, salt, and pepper before roasting for next-level flavor.

12. Chicken Fajita Bake

Why It Rocks

All the fajita fun in one pan. No need to hover over a sizzling skillet—pop it in the oven, and done.

Ingredients (Serves 3–4)

- 1 lb chicken breast, sliced
- 2 bell peppers, sliced
- 1 onion, sliced
- 1 tbsp olive oil
- 1 packet (or homemade) fajita seasoning
- Salt, pepper

Method

1. **Preheat** oven to 400°F (200°C).
2. **Toss** chicken, peppers, onion with oil, seasoning.
3. **Spread** on a sheet pan, bake ~20–25 minutes until chicken is done.

Pro Tip

Serve with warm whole-wheat tortillas or on top of greens for a low-carb fajita salad.

13. Beef & Veggie Kebabs

Why It Rocks
Skewers of marinated beef and colorful veggies are fun to eat and deliver a big protein payoff. Grill or broil for that smoky char.

Ingredients (Makes ~6–8 kebabs)

- 1 lb lean steak (sirloin or top round), cut into cubes
- 2 cups mixed bell peppers, onions, zucchini (cubed)
- Marinade: 2 tbsp low-sodium soy sauce, 1 tbsp olive oil, 1 tbsp lemon juice, garlic powder, pepper

Method

1. **Marinate** steak cubes at least 30 minutes.
2. **Thread** steak and veggies alternately onto skewers.
3. **Grill** or broil ~10–12 minutes, turning halfway.

Pro Tip
Soak wooden skewers in water first so they don't burn. Also, feel free to toss pineapple chunks on there for a sweet-savory twist.

14. Turkey & Quinoa Stuffed Peppers

Why It Rocks
Lean turkey, high-protein quinoa, and colorful peppers—this combo leaves you full without that heavy, bloated feeling.

Ingredients (Makes 4 peppers)

- ½ lb ground turkey
- 1 cup cooked quinoa
- 4 bell peppers, tops cut off, seeds removed
- 1 cup tomato sauce
- Salt, pepper, Italian seasoning

Method

1. **Preheat** oven to 375°F (190°C).
2. **Brown** turkey in a skillet, stir in quinoa, sauce, and seasonings.
3. **Fill** peppers with the mixture, place in a baking dish.
4. **Bake** ~20 minutes until peppers are tender and stuffing is hot.

15. Lemon Garlic Tilapia with Roasted Broccoli

Why It Rocks
Tilapia is super lean, and the lemon-garlic combo keeps it anything but boring. Roasted broccoli adds fiber and a hint of crispness.

Ingredients (Serves 2)

- 2 tilapia fillets (5–6 oz each)
- 1 lemon (zest + juice)
- 2 cloves garlic, minced
- 2 cups broccoli florets
- 1 tbsp olive oil
- Salt, pepper

Method

1. **Preheat** oven to 400°F (200°C).
2. **Toss** broccoli with half the olive oil, salt, pepper; place on a baking sheet.
3. **Whisk** remaining oil with lemon zest, juice, garlic—brush over tilapia.
4. **Bake** tilapia on the same sheet (if space allows) ~10–12 minutes until fish flakes.

Pro Tip
Want a carb source? Toss a sweet potato in there or serve with a side of rice if you're bulking.

16. Chili Lime Chicken & Cauliflower Rice

Why It Rocks
Cauliflower rice kills the carb count but not the flavor. Chili-lime chicken packs a tangy punch that keeps you excited to eat clean.

Ingredients (Serves 2–3)

- 1 lb chicken breast, cut into strips
- Marinade: juice of 1 lime, 1 tsp chili powder, 1 tsp olive oil, salt, pepper
- 3 cups cauliflower rice (store-bought or homemade)
- 1 cup mixed peppers, diced

Method

1. **Marinate** chicken in chili-lime mix ~20 minutes.
2. **Cook** chicken in a skillet until browned. Remove and set aside.
3. **Sauté** peppers, then add cauliflower rice, season with salt, pepper.
4. **Combine** chicken, stir, and serve hot.

Pro Tip

Don't overcook cauliflower rice—it can turn mushy fast. Keep it al dente for the best texture.

17. Big-Batch Turkey & Veggie Chili

Why It Rocks

Similar to a standard chili, but we're cranking up the volume with extra veggies, ground turkey, and bold spices. Perfect for leftovers.

Ingredients (Serves ~6)

- 1 lb ground turkey
- 1 onion, diced
- 2 cups mixed diced veggies (bell peppers, zucchini, carrots)
- 1 can black beans, 1 can kidney beans (drained)
- 1 can (14–15 oz) crushed tomatoes
- 2 tbsp chili powder, 1 tsp cumin, salt, pepper

Method

1. **Brown** turkey and onion in a large pot.
2. **Add** veggies, beans, tomatoes, and spices.
3. **Simmer** 20–30 minutes, stirring occasionally.

Pro Tip

Freeze extra portions for days you need a no-brainer, high-protein dinner. It's a lifesaver.

18. Ginger-Soy Ground Beef & Green Beans

Why It Rocks

A simple stir-fry that's quick, lean, and loaded with ginger-soy flavor. Green beans add a satisfying crunch.

Ingredients (Serves 2–3)

- 1 lb lean ground beef (90% or better)
- 2 cups fresh or frozen green beans
- 1 tbsp grated fresh ginger, 2 cloves garlic (minced)
- 2 tbsp low-sodium soy sauce or tamari
- 1 tsp cornstarch + 1 tbsp water

Method

1. **Cook** ground beef in a skillet until browned; drain any excess fat.
2. **Add** ginger, garlic, soy sauce.
3. **Stir** in green beans; cook until tender-crisp.
4. **Thicken** with cornstarch slurry if desired.

Pro Tip
Serve over brown rice or cauliflower rice—depends on your carb goals. Sriracha drizzle is always welcome.

19. Chicken & Broccoli Alfredo (Lightened Up)

Why It Rocks
Alfredo sauce usually screams "heavy cream"—we're using Greek yogurt and a bit of low-fat milk to keep it creamy without the guilt.

Ingredients (Serves 2)

- 1 chicken breast (8–10 oz), cubed
- 2 cups broccoli florets
- 1 cup whole-wheat penne (or high-protein pasta)
- ½ cup low-fat milk
- ¼ cup Greek yogurt
- 2 cloves garlic, minced
- 2 tbsp Parmesan cheese, salt, pepper

Method

1. **Cook** pasta according to package. Add broccoli in the last 2 minutes.
2. **Sauté** chicken in a pan until browned.
3. **Whisk** milk, yogurt, garlic, Parmesan in a small bowl; season with salt, pepper.
4. **Combine** pasta, broccoli, chicken, and sauce in the pan. Heat gently.

Pro Tip
Don't boil the sauce or it may separate. Keep the heat low to maintain that creamy texture.

20. Baked Garlic-Parmesan Turkey Cutlets

Why It Rocks
Crispy outside, juicy inside. A lighter alternative to fried chicken cutlets, with a major protein payoff.

Ingredients (Makes ~4 cutlets)

- 1 lb turkey breast cutlets
- ½ cup whole-wheat breadcrumbs
- 2 tbsp grated Parmesan
- 1 tsp garlic powder, salt, pepper
- 1 egg + 1 egg white, beaten

Method

1. **Preheat** oven to 400°F (200°C).
2. **Combine** breadcrumbs, Parmesan, garlic powder, salt, pepper in a shallow dish.
3. **Dip** each cutlet in beaten egg, then coat in breadcrumb mix.
4. **Bake** on a greased sheet ~15–20 minutes until golden.

Pro Tip
Pair with roasted veggies or a simple side salad. If you're bulking, add a serving of brown rice or whole-grain pasta on the side.

Keep the Flavor Rolling

These **20 hearty dinner options** prove you can **pack the protein**, stay lean, and still tear into a plate bursting with taste every single night. Whether you're a grill junkie, a stew lover, or a fan of one-pan wonders, there's something here to keep your macros in line and your cravings satisfied.

Next up: If you're still hungry for more, buckle up—**20** more knockout recipes are on the way. But first, get in that kitchen and see how these beauties fit into your meal plan. When you're ready for Round 2, you know where to find it!

21. Garlic-Herb Turkey Burgers with Portobello Buns

Why It Rocks
Say goodbye to carb-heavy buns and hello to savory portobello mushrooms. Juicy turkey burgers that keep you lean and loaded with flavor.

Ingredients (Makes ~4 burgers)

- 1 lb ground turkey (93% lean or better)
- 2 cloves garlic, minced
- 1 tsp dried herbs (rosemary, thyme, or Italian seasoning)
- Salt, pepper
- 8 portobello mushroom caps (stem removed)

Method

1. **Preheat** oven or grill to ~400°F (200°C).
2. **Mix** turkey, garlic, herbs, salt, pepper. Form into 4 patties.
3. **Grill or bake** portobello caps brushed with a little oil, ~5–7 minutes per side.
4. **Cook** turkey patties until internal temp hits 165°F (74°C).
5. **Assemble** using mushroom caps as buns.

Pro Tip
Top with sliced tomato, lettuce, and a smear of Greek yogurt or mustard. Extra veggies, no wasted calories.

22. Blackened Tilapia Tacos with Slaw

Why It Rocks
Bold blackening seasoning and crunchy slaw bring the heat—and the protein. Skip the fried fish for a lean, tasty taco you won't regret.

Ingredients (Makes ~6 tacos)

- 1 lb tilapia fillets
- 1 tbsp blackening or Cajun seasoning
- 6 small corn or whole-wheat tortillas
- 2 cups shredded cabbage or slaw mix
- 1 tbsp lime juice
- Salt, pepper

Method

1. **Season** tilapia fillets with blackening spice.
2. **Cook** in a hot skillet (sprayed lightly) ~3–4 minutes per side.
3. **Toss** slaw with lime juice, salt, pepper.
4. **Assemble** tacos: tilapia chunks + slaw on tortillas.

Pro Tip
Amp up the flavor with a quick sauce: Greek yogurt + hot sauce + a dash of lime. Drizzle that bad boy on top.

23. Sheet-Pan Lemon-Herb Chicken & Asparagus

Why It Rocks
Chicken and veggies, all on one pan. Clean-up is a joke, and the lemon-herb combo pops with fresh flavor.

Ingredients (Serves 2–3)

- 1 lb chicken breast or tenders
- 1 bunch asparagus (trimmed)
- 1 lemon (zest + juice)
- 1 tbsp olive oil
- Salt, pepper, dried herbs (thyme, basil, or rosemary)

Method

1. **Preheat** oven to 400°F (200°C).
2. **Mix** olive oil, lemon juice/zest, herbs, salt, pepper.
3. **Coat** chicken and asparagus with the mixture on a sheet pan.
4. **Roast** ~15–20 minutes until chicken hits 165°F (74°C).

Pro Tip
Add cherry tomatoes or thinly sliced red onion to bring an extra punch of color and flavor.

24. High-Protein Kung Pao Chicken

Why It Rocks
A leaner spin on the takeout classic. No greasy battered chicken—just bold, spicy sauce and crunchy peanuts if your macros allow.

Ingredients (Serves 2–3)

- 1 lb chicken breast, cubed
- 2 cups chopped bell peppers, onions, zucchini
- 1 tbsp soy sauce, 1 tbsp rice vinegar, 1 tbsp chili sauce
- 1 tsp cornstarch mixed with 1 tbsp water (for thickening)
- Handful of peanuts (optional, or sub cashews)

Method

1. **Cook** chicken in a skillet, season with salt, pepper. Remove when browned.
2. **Stir-fry** veggies, then add sauce ingredients plus cornstarch slurry.
3. **Return** chicken to pan, coat in sauce.
4. **Sprinkle** peanuts if you're feeling it.

Pro Tip

Dial the spiciness up or down by adjusting chili sauce. Serve over cauliflower rice or brown rice based on your carb needs.

25. Protein-Packed Egg Roll in a Bowl

Why It Rocks

All the savory goodness of an egg roll, minus the deep-fried wrapper. Lean ground meat + crunchy slaw = instant dinner win.

Ingredients (Serves 2–3)

- 1 lb lean ground pork, turkey, or chicken
- 3 cups coleslaw mix (shredded cabbage, carrots)
- 2 tbsp low-sodium soy sauce
- 1 tsp sesame oil (optional)
- 2 cloves garlic, minced
- 1 tsp grated ginger

Method

1. **Brown** meat in a skillet, drain any excess fat.
2. **Add** garlic, ginger, soy sauce, sesame oil.
3. **Stir** in coleslaw mix; cook until just wilted.
4. **Season** with salt, pepper to taste.

Pro Tip

Top with a drizzle of sriracha or chili flakes if you want an extra kick. This dish also reheats like a champ.

26. Roasted Pork Loin with Veggie Medley

Why It Rocks

Pork loin is ultra-lean when trimmed right. Roast it with a colorful spread of veggies for a simple, nutrient-packed meal.

Ingredients (Serves 3–4)

- 1 lb pork loin, trimmed
- 2 cups mixed veggies (carrots, onions, Brussels sprouts)
- 1 tbsp olive oil
- Salt, pepper, rosemary

Method

1. **Preheat** oven to 375°F (190°C).
2. **Season** pork with salt, pepper, rosemary; place in roasting pan.
3. **Toss** veggies in olive oil, salt, pepper, arrange around pork.
4. **Roast** ~25–30 minutes until pork hits 145°F (63°C). Rest 5 minutes, slice.

Pro Tip

If you want a sauce, whisk a little low-sodium broth with a splash of balsamic and reduce in a small pan. Drizzle at serving.

27. Mediterranean Chicken Skillet

Why It Rocks

Tomatoes, olives, feta, and lean chicken breast combine for a salty, tangy flavor bomb straight from the Mediterranean.

Ingredients (Serves 2–3)

- 1 lb chicken breast, cubed
- 1 can diced tomatoes (14–15 oz, no salt added)
- ½ cup pitted olives, sliced (black or kalamata)
- 2 cloves garlic, minced
- ¼ cup feta crumbles (optional)
- Italian seasoning, salt, pepper

Method

1. **Cook** chicken in a large skillet with olive oil, garlic, salt, pepper.
2. **Add** tomatoes, olives, Italian seasoning. Simmer ~10 minutes.

3. **Sprinkle** feta before serving, let it warm up.

Pro Tip
Serve over quinoa or whole-wheat couscous to keep that Mediterranean vibe strong and add extra protein/fiber.

28. Lentil Shepherd's Pie

Why It Rocks
Who says you need ground beef for a proper shepherd's pie? Lentils provide serious protein and fiber, topped with mashed potatoes for that comforting finish.

Ingredients (Serves 3–4)

- 1 cup lentils (rinsed)
- 1 onion, diced
- 2 carrots, diced
- 2 cups low-sodium vegetable broth
- Mashed potatoes (from 3–4 potatoes, or sub sweet potatoes)
- Salt, pepper, thyme

Method

1. **Sauté** onion, carrot in a skillet.
2. **Add** lentils, broth, thyme; simmer until lentils are tender (~20 minutes).
3. **Spread** lentil mixture in a baking dish, top with mashed potatoes.
4. **Bake** at 375°F (190°C) ~15 minutes or until potatoes brown slightly.

Pro Tip
Looking to up the protein? Mix half lentils, half ground turkey, and proceed as usual.

29. Salsa Verde Chicken Enchiladas

Why It Rocks
A lighter spin on enchiladas that still nails that cheesy, saucy goodness. Salsa verde keeps things tangy and fresh.

Ingredients (Makes ~6 enchiladas)

- 1 lb shredded chicken (breast meat)
- 6 whole-wheat tortillas

- 1 cup salsa verde
- ½ cup shredded low-fat cheese
- 1 onion, diced
- Cumin, salt, pepper

Method

1. **Preheat** oven to 375°F (190°C).
2. **Mix** shredded chicken, onion, cumin, a splash of salsa verde.
3. **Fill** tortillas, roll them up, place seam-side down in a baking dish.
4. **Pour** remaining salsa verde on top, sprinkle cheese.
5. **Bake** ~15–20 minutes until cheese melts.

Pro Tip

Serve with a side of Greek yogurt or guac if your macros allow. Jalapeños for the heat-seekers.

30. Marinated Flank Steak & Roasted Sweet Potatoes

Why It Rocks

Flank steak is lean when trimmed right, and a simple marinade turns it into a flavor powerhouse. Sweet potatoes round out the complex carbs.

Ingredients (Serves 3–4)

- 1 lb flank steak, trimmed
- Marinade: 2 tbsp low-sodium soy sauce, 1 tbsp olive oil, 1 tbsp balsamic vinegar, garlic, black pepper
- 2 medium sweet potatoes, cut into wedges
- Salt, pepper, paprika

Method

1. **Marinate** steak at least 30 minutes (overnight is golden).
2. **Toss** sweet potato wedges with olive oil, salt, pepper, paprika; bake at 400°F (200°C) ~20–25 mins.
3. **Grill or broil** steak ~5–6 minutes per side for medium rare.
4. **Rest** steak 5 minutes, slice thin against the grain.

Pro Tip

Add roasted Brussels sprouts or asparagus if you need more veggies without adding many calories.

31. Baked Cod in Tomato Sauce

Why It Rocks

Mild cod soaks up a chunky tomato sauce for a light but hearty meal. Toss in olives or capers if you want a Mediterranean punch.

Ingredients (Serves 2)

- 2 cod fillets (~5–6 oz each)
- 1 can diced tomatoes (14–15 oz)
- 2 cloves garlic, minced
- 1 small onion, diced
- 1 tsp dried basil, salt, pepper

Method

1. **Sauté** onion, garlic in an ovenproof skillet.
2. **Add** diced tomatoes, basil, salt, pepper; let simmer 5 minutes.
3. **Nestle** cod fillets in sauce.
4. **Bake** at 375°F (190°C) ~10–12 minutes until cod flakes.

Pro Tip

Serve with a side of whole-wheat pasta, quinoa, or just spoon that sauce over some roasted veggies for a lower-carb option.

32. Slow-Cooker Chicken & Veggie Curry

Why It Rocks

Toss everything in the slow cooker, go about your day, and come home to a spicy, creamy curry loaded with lean chicken.

Ingredients (Serves 4)

- 1 lb chicken breast, cubed
- 2 cups mixed veggies (carrots, peppers, onions)
- 1 can (13–14 oz) light coconut milk
- 2 tbsp curry powder or curry paste (to taste)
- Salt, pepper

Method

1. **Add** chicken, veggies, coconut milk, curry powder/paste, salt, pepper to slow cooker.
2. **Cook** on low ~6–7 hours (or high ~3–4 hours) until chicken is tender.

Pro Tip

Serve over brown rice, or skip the grains if you're going low-carb. Garnish with fresh cilantro if you're feeling fancy.

33. High-Protein Chicken Alfredo Bake

Why It Rocks

Similar to #19 but baked in a casserole style, so you can portion it out for multiple nights. Greek yogurt keeps it creamy.

Ingredients (Serves 3–4)

- 1 lb chicken breast, cubed
- 2 cups whole-wheat pasta (penne or rotini)
- 1 cup steamed broccoli florets
- Sauce: ½ cup low-fat milk, ½ cup Greek yogurt, 2 cloves garlic, 2 tbsp Parmesan
- Salt, pepper

Method

1. **Cook** pasta and chicken separately.
2. **Steam** broccoli.
3. **Blend** sauce ingredients in a small bowl (milk, yogurt, garlic, Parmesan, seasonings).
4. **Combine** pasta, chicken, broccoli, and sauce in a baking dish.
5. **Bake** at 375°F (190°C) ~15–20 minutes.

Pro Tip

Top with a sprinkle of low-fat mozzarella if you want that cheese pull effect.

34. Moroccan-Style Turkey Meatloaf

Why It Rocks

Spiced with cumin, paprika, and maybe a pinch of cinnamon. It's a twist on meatloaf that's far from bland.

Ingredients (Serves 3–4)

- 1 lb ground turkey
- 1 egg
- ½ cup breadcrumbs (whole-wheat if possible)
- 1 tsp cumin, 1 tsp paprika, ¼ tsp cinnamon, salt, pepper

- 1 onion, finely diced

Method

1. **Preheat** oven to 375°F (190°C).
2. **Combine** turkey, egg, breadcrumbs, spices, onion in a bowl.
3. **Shape** into a loaf, place in a baking pan.
4. **Bake** ~25–30 minutes until internal temp is 165°F (74°C).

Pro Tip
Serve with roasted veggies or a chickpea salad for a full Moroccan-inspired meal.

35. Spicy Peanut Chicken Stir-Fry

Why It Rocks
A killer combo of peanuts, chili, and lean chicken. Adjust peanut butter usage to fit your macro needs without sacrificing taste.

Ingredients (Serves 2–3)

- 1 lb chicken breast, cubed
- 2 cups stir-fry veggies (bell peppers, onions, carrots)
- 1 tbsp peanut butter (natural)
- 1 tbsp low-sodium soy sauce
- 1 tsp chili paste or sriracha
- 1 tsp grated ginger (optional)

Method

1. **Cook** chicken in a skillet; remove once browned.
2. **Stir-fry** veggies.
3. **Combine** peanut butter, soy sauce, chili paste, ginger in a small bowl.
4. **Toss** chicken back in with sauce. Coat everything.

Pro Tip
Serve over brown rice or cauliflower rice. Top with crushed peanuts if you can afford the extra fats in your macros.

36. High-Protein Vegan Chili Mac

Why It Rocks
Chili + mac n' cheese = comfort meal. We're swapping in a vegan cheese sauce and beans for a protein boost that's friendly to plant-based eaters.

Ingredients (Serves 3–4)

- 1 cup whole-wheat or chickpea pasta (elbows)
- 1 can black beans, drained
- 1 can diced tomatoes (14–15 oz)
- 1 tbsp chili powder, 1 tsp cumin
- Vegan cheese sauce (store-bought or homemade cashew-based)
- Optional: bell peppers, onions

Method

1. **Cook** pasta according to package.
2. **Combine** beans, tomatoes, chili powder, cumin in a saucepan; simmer.
3. **Stir** in pasta, then fold in vegan cheese sauce.
4. **Heat** gently, season with salt, pepper.

Pro Tip
Add textured vegetable protein (TVP) or beyond-meat crumbles if you want even more plant-based protein.

37. Shredded BBQ Chicken Sweet Potato

Why It Rocks
A comfort-food vibe: sweet potato stuffed with saucy shredded chicken. High protein, complex carbs—filling and flavorful.

Ingredients (Serves 2)

- 2 medium sweet potatoes
- 1 chicken breast (~8 oz), cooked and shredded
- ¼ cup low-sugar BBQ sauce
- Salt, pepper

Method

1. **Bake** or microwave sweet potatoes until fork-tender.
2. **Mix** shredded chicken with BBQ sauce, warm in a skillet or microwave.

3. **Split** potatoes open, stuff with chicken.

Pro Tip
Add a spoonful of Greek yogurt, chopped green onions, or even diced jalapeños for extra flair.

38. Creamy Garlic Shrimp & Spinach

Why It Rocks
Low-carb, protein-heavy, and seriously creamy without going overboard on the fat. Perfect for a quick 15-minute dinner.

Ingredients (Serves 2)

- 1 lb shrimp, peeled & deveined
- 2 cups fresh spinach
- 2 cloves garlic, minced
- ½ cup low-fat milk (or almond milk)
- 1 tbsp cornstarch + 2 tbsp water (slurry)
- Salt, pepper

Method

1. **Sauté** garlic in a pan; add shrimp, salt, pepper. Cook until pink.
2. **Pour** in milk, bring to a simmer.
3. **Stir** in cornstarch slurry to thicken.
4. **Add** spinach; let it wilt.

Pro Tip
Serve over zucchini noodles or whole-wheat pasta, depending on your carb goals.

39. Big-Batch Chicken & Veggie Soup

Why It Rocks
Light yet filling, this soup is a must for meal-preppers. Packed with lean chicken and enough veggies to keep you satisfied.

Ingredients (Makes a big pot, ~6 servings)

- 1 lb chicken breast, diced
- 1 onion, chopped
- 2 carrots, sliced

- 2 celery stalks, sliced
- 6 cups low-sodium chicken broth
- Salt, pepper, Italian herbs

Method

1. **Sauté** chicken, onion in a large pot.
2. **Add** carrots, celery, broth, herbs.
3. **Simmer** ~20–25 minutes.

Pro Tip
Throw in a handful of whole-wheat pasta or brown rice if you need extra carbs. This soup also freezes well.

40. Zesty Citrus Turkey Cutlets

Why It Rocks
Bright, tangy citrus marinade infuses turkey cutlets with flavor. Quick-cooking, lean, and easy on the cleanup.

Ingredients (Serves 2–3)

- 1 lb turkey breast cutlets
- Marinade: juice of 1 orange + 1 lime, 1 tbsp olive oil, pinch of chili flakes, salt, pepper
- Optional sides: roasted broccoli or cauliflower, brown rice

Method

1. **Marinate** turkey in citrus mix ~20 minutes.
2. **Cook** in a hot skillet or grill ~4–5 minutes per side (depends on thickness).
3. **Rest** cutlets a couple of minutes, then slice.

Pro Tip
Brush extra marinade on during cooking for bolder flavor—just make sure any marinade that touched raw poultry is cooked thoroughly.

You're All Set

That wraps up the **40** total **Nighttime Knockouts**—**20** here plus the **20** from before—each packing enough **lean protein**, **explosive flavor**, and **muscle-building mojo** to end your day strong. Now you can go to bed knowing your body's got exactly what it needs to recover, rebuild, and wake up **ready to conquer. Let's call it a day—but a damn good one.**

CHAPTER 7: SNACK ATTACK—HIGH-PROTEIN BITES TO KEEP YOU GOING

When cravings strike, don't cave—attack. Stock up on these simple, badass snacks to knock hunger on its ass any time of day.

Let's cut the crap: when hunger hits like a raging bull, you've got two choices—cower and cave to the nearest trashy vending-machine special, or **step up** and demolish those cravings before they put your progress in a chokehold. This chapter is the difference between **slaying** your mid-afternoon slump and stumbling through the rest of your day like a half-dead zombie. If that sounds dramatic, good. Because if you're serious about building muscle and keeping your energy on lock, you'd better start taking your snack game **seriously**.

No more whining about how you "don't have time" to make decent snacks. You had time to scroll social media, right? Thought so. The **high-protein bites** in this chapter practically **make themselves**. They're so stupidly simple that even the busiest soul on Earth can whip 'em up. Throw a couple in your desk drawer, your gym bag, or your fridge at home, and watch how quickly you crush those "I'm starving" moments—**before** they sucker-punch your diet.

And let's be crystal clear: if you're still shoving chips, cookies, or candy bars down your throat whenever a craving kicks in, you're basically flushing your hard-earned gains down the toilet. You can blame "lack of options" all you want, but that's total BS—and you know it. By the time you finish this chapter, you'll have a stack of **no-excuses** snack ideas that are so loaded with protein, they'll make your taste buds cheer and your muscles thank you.

Why Snacks Even Matter

"Do I really need high-protein snacks?" You better believe it. Between meals, your body still needs **quality** fuel to ward off catabolic breakdown (that's fancy talk for your muscles going bye-bye) and to keep your blood sugar from flatlining. Skip decent snacks, and you risk turning into a hangry monster who'd kill for a chocolate bar—and you might just sabotage the solid progress you've made. These recipes are about **staying ahead** of that hunger curve, so you're not wandering into a convenience store ready to devour the first bag of junk you see.

Make Hunger Beg for Mercy

The snacks in this chapter range from **grab-and-go** to **mix-it-up** quickies, from **sweet** to **savory**, ensuring you never get bored and never have to default to leftover doughnuts in the break room. Each one delivers a **punch** of protein—enough to keep your stomach from growling and your cravings on ice until your next meal. So when that wave of hunger tries to knock you down, you **knock it down first**, like the unstoppable machine you are.

Ready to Stock Up?

Check your fridge, pantry, and desk drawers. If you see more packages of candy and random junk than actual **muscle-friendly** snacks, you've got homework. Rid that crap, and replace it with real options that don't sabotage your macros. There's **no room** for half-measures if you want serious results—being unprepared is just an invitation for your cravings to walk all over you.

So here's the bottom line: **nobody** is too busy, too tired, or too clueless to stock up on these easy, badass snacks. It's time to **attack** your hunger before it attacks you. Slam down a protein-packed bite, refuel, and get back to crushing your day like the unstoppable force you were meant to be. Because around here, we don't **give** cravings a chance—we kill them on sight. Bring on the **Snack Attack**, and let's keep those gains rolling!

Recipes Included: 20 quick-fix snacks (protein bars, meatless bites, on-the-go shakes)

Below are **20** quick, no-excuses snack options that are **protein-rich**, **stupidly simple**, and made to **destroy** hunger before it even has a shot. Each one follows the same format—**Why It Rocks**, **Ingredients**, **Method**, and a **Pro Tip**—so you can grab what you need and get back to annihilating your day. Let's go!

1. DIY Protein Bars

Why It Rocks
Skip the overpriced, sugar-loaded bars at the store. These are **customizable**, so you know exactly what's going into your macros.

Ingredients (Makes ~8 bars)

- 2 cups rolled oats (blended into flour, if you prefer)
- 1 cup whey or plant-based protein powder
- ¼ cup nut butter (peanut, almond)
- 2–3 tbsp honey or maple syrup (optional for sweetness)
- ½ cup milk (low-fat or almond milk)
- Pinch of salt, cinnamon (optional)

Method

1. **Mix** oats, protein powder, nut butter in a bowl.

2. **Add** milk gradually until it forms a dough-like consistency.
3. **Press** into a pan lined with parchment, refrigerate for at least an hour.
4. **Slice** into bars.

Pro Tip
Throw in chopped nuts or dark chocolate chips if you want texture or extra flavor (just watch your macros).

2. Protein-Packed Cottage Cheese Dip

Why It Rocks
Cottage cheese is already high in protein, and with a few flavor boosts, it becomes a **tasty** dip for veggies or whole-grain crackers.

Ingredients (Serves ~2)

- 1 cup low-fat cottage cheese
- 2 tbsp Greek yogurt (optional for extra creaminess)
- 1 clove garlic, minced (or ½ tsp garlic powder)
- 1 tsp dried herbs (dill, basil, or Italian seasoning)
- Salt, pepper

Method

1. **Blend** cottage cheese, yogurt, garlic, herbs.
2. **Adjust** seasonings to taste.
3. **Serve** with carrot sticks, cucumber rounds, or whole-grain crackers.

Pro Tip
Double the batch and store in airtight containers—it'll keep for a few days, so you can grab it on the fly.

3. Greek Yogurt Parfait Cups

Why It Rocks
Layered Greek yogurt, fruit, and maybe a sprinkle of granola gives you a **dessert-like** snack without tanking your macros.

Ingredients (Makes 2 cups)

- 2 cups plain Greek yogurt

- 1 cup fresh berries (strawberries, blueberries, raspberries)
- Sweetener of choice (honey, stevia)
- ¼ cup high-protein granola (optional)

Method

1. **Layer** yogurt and berries in a jar or cup.
2. **Drizzle** sweetener if needed.
3. **Top** with granola for crunch.

Pro Tip

Prep these in mason jars for an easy grab-and-go snack—just add granola right before eating so it stays crisp.

4. High-Protein Trail Mix

Why It Rocks

Store-bought trail mix can be a sugar bomb. Make your own with **quality** nuts, seeds, and a hint of sweetness for an energy boost.

Ingredients (Makes ~4 servings)

- ½ cup almonds
- ½ cup peanuts (or cashews)
- ¼ cup pumpkin seeds or sunflower seeds
- ¼ cup unsweetened dried fruit (cranberries, raisins) (optional)
- 2 tbsp dark chocolate chips (optional, but hey—treat yourself)

Method

1. **Combine** all ingredients in a ziplock bag or container.
2. **Shake** it up to mix.

Pro Tip

Portion it into small snack bags to avoid mindless munching. This stuff can add up fast if you lose track.

5. Tuna or Salmon Pouches

Why It Rocks
They're **already cooked**, zero prep required, and high in protein with virtually no extra junk. Perfect "rip and eat" snack.

Ingredients

- 1 pouch tuna or salmon (usually ~2.6–3 oz)
- Optional add-ons: hot sauce, mustard, Greek yogurt

Method

1. **Open** the pouch.
2. **Eat**. Done.

Pro Tip
Keep a few pouches at your desk or in your gym bag. Mix with a spoonful of Greek yogurt or mustard for moisture if needed.

6. No-Bake Protein Bites

Why It Rocks
Think of these as bite-sized energy balls that taste like dessert but pack a protein punch to shut hunger down.

Ingredients (Makes ~12–15 bites)

- 1 cup oats
- ½ cup nut butter (peanut, almond)
- ½ cup protein powder (whey or plant-based)
- 1–2 tbsp honey or maple syrup
- 1–2 tbsp water (if needed for binding)

Method

1. **Combine** oats, protein powder, nut butter, sweetener.
2. **Add** water if it's too dry.
3. **Roll** into bite-sized balls.
4. **Refrigerate** in an airtight container.

Pro Tip
Add shredded coconut, flax seeds, or mini chocolate chips for extra texture—just keep macros in check.

7. Sliced Turkey & Cheese Roll-Ups

Why It Rocks
No bread, no nonsense—just lean turkey slices wrapped around cheese. It's practically lunch in miniature form.

Ingredients (Makes ~4 roll-ups)

- 4 slices turkey breast (deli style)
- 4 sticks low-fat mozzarella or 4 slices reduced-fat cheese
- Optional: mustard or a thin layer of hummus

Method

1. **Spread** mustard or hummus on each turkey slice.
2. **Place** cheese on top, roll it up tight.
3. **Stash** in a container or eat right away.

Pro Tip
Toss a few spinach leaves or thin cucumber slices inside for a sneaky veggie boost.

8. Protein Shake on the Run

Why It Rocks
You can't beat the simplicity of a **shake** when you're strapped for time. Instant protein hit, no cooking involved.

Ingredients

- 1 scoop whey or plant-based protein
- 8–12 oz water, milk, or almond milk
- Optional add-ins: spinach, frozen fruit, nut butter

Method

1. **Dump** protein powder in a shaker bottle.
2. **Add** liquid.

3. **Shake** until blended.

Pro Tip
Keep a spare shaker bottle and protein serving in a ziplock bag at work or in your car. Crisis averted.

9. Roasted Chickpeas

Why It Rocks
Crunchy, savory, and full of protein and fiber. Satisfies that "chip" craving without going off the rails.

Ingredients (Makes ~2 cups)

- 1 can chickpeas, drained, rinsed, and patted dry
- 1 tbsp olive oil
- Seasonings: salt, pepper, paprika, chili powder—your call

Method

1. **Preheat** oven to 400°F (200°C).
2. **Toss** chickpeas with oil and seasonings.
3. **Roast** on a baking sheet ~20–30 minutes, shaking halfway.

Pro Tip
Let them cool completely if you want maximum crunch. Store in an airtight container for a day or two.

10. Beef Jerky or Biltong

Why It Rocks
Portable, lean protein that doesn't require refrigeration. Just watch for low-sugar, low-sodium varieties to keep it clean.

Ingredients

- 1 bag of beef jerky or biltong (around 2–3 oz)

Method

1. **Open** the bag.

2. **Chew** on delicious protein.

Pro Tip
Check labels for sugar content—some brands go overboard with sweet marinades. You want protein, not a candy bar in disguise.

11. Hard-Boiled Eggs

Why It Rocks
Classic and reliable. Hard-boiling a bunch at once means you have protein bombs ready to go in the fridge at all times.

Ingredients

- However many eggs you want to boil

Method

1. **Place** eggs in a pot, cover with water.
2. **Bring** to a rolling boil, then reduce heat to a gentle boil ~9–12 minutes depending on how firm you like 'em.
3. **Cool** in ice water, peel, store.

Pro Tip
Sprinkle with salt, pepper, or everything bagel seasoning. And don't let the old egg smell scare you off—your gains will thank you.

12. Edamame Pods

Why It Rocks
High-protein soybeans you can steam or microwave in minutes. Tasty with just a little salt or spice.

Ingredients

- 1 bag frozen edamame pods (in the shell)
- Salt, chili flakes, or soy sauce (optional)

Method

1. **Steam or microwave** according to package.

2. **Season** lightly.

Pro Tip
Eat the beans straight from the pods—keeps your hands busy and helps you slow down so you don't inhale them too fast.

13. Mini Tuna Patties

Why It Rocks
Little tuna cakes you can make in bulk and stash in the fridge. Great for quick bites that pack a protein punch.

Ingredients (Makes ~6 patties)

- 2 cans tuna in water, drained
- 1 egg
- ¼ cup breadcrumbs (whole-wheat if possible)
- Seasonings: garlic powder, onion powder, salt, pepper

Method

1. **Combine** tuna, egg, breadcrumbs, seasonings in a bowl.
2. **Form** small patties.
3. **Pan-sear** on a lightly oiled skillet, ~3–4 mins per side.

Pro Tip
Top with a spoonful of Greek yogurt or mustard for extra moisture. They're surprisingly good cold, too.

14. Protein Mug Cake

Why It Rocks
Dessert-like snack that ditches the guilt. Perfect if you want something sweet but protein-heavy.

Ingredients (Makes 1 mug cake)

- 1 scoop protein powder (chocolate or vanilla)
- 1 tbsp cocoa powder (if using chocolate protein, you can skip this)
- 1 egg or 2 egg whites
- 1–2 tbsp milk (or almond milk)
- Sweetener to taste

Method

1. **Mix** everything in a microwave-safe mug.
2. **Microwave** ~45–60 seconds, watch so it doesn't overflow.

Pro Tip
Microwave times vary—don't overcook or it'll turn rubbery. Top with a dab of Greek yogurt or peanut butter if you need extra indulgence.

15. Apple Slices with Almond Butter

Why It Rocks
A classic sweet-and-salty snack that hits the spot. Almond butter adds healthy fats and protein, apples bring fiber.

Ingredients

- 1 apple, sliced
- 1–2 tbsp almond butter (or peanut butter)

Method

1. **Slice** the apple.
2. **Dip** in almond butter.
3. **Devour**.

Pro Tip
Want more protein? Add a sprinkle of protein powder to the almond butter and stir it in. It'll thicken, but it gets the job done.

16. Turkey or Chicken Jerky Sticks

Why It Rocks
Similar to beef jerky but often leaner. Perfect for those moments you need meat but can't cook.

Ingredients

- A pack of turkey or chicken jerky sticks (low-sodium, low-sugar)

Method

1. **Tear** open the pack.

2. **Munch** until hunger says uncle.

Pro Tip
Keep an eye on the sodium content. Too much salt can make you balloon with water retention.

17. Protein Hot Chocolate

Why It Rocks
Warm, chocolatey goodness that also happens to give you a protein boost. Ideal for cold days or late-night cravings.

Ingredients (Serves 1)

- 1 cup low-fat milk or almond milk
- 1 scoop chocolate protein powder
- 1 tsp cocoa powder (optional)
- Sweetener to taste

Method

1. **Warm** milk in a saucepan or microwave.
2. **Whisk** in protein powder, cocoa, and sweetener.
3. **Heat** gently, stirring often. Don't let it boil.

Pro Tip
Top with a tiny dollop of whipped cream or mini marshmallows if macros allow—life's short, live a little.

18. Protein Popcorn

Why It Rocks
Popcorn is high in volume, so it fills you up, and adding a light protein coating makes it a stealthy macro win.

Ingredients (Makes ~2 servings)

- 4 cups air-popped popcorn (no butter)
- 1 scoop unflavored or lightly flavored protein powder
- 1 tbsp melted coconut oil or a light spray of cooking oil
- Salt or seasoning of choice

Method

1. **Air-pop** popcorn.
2. **Lightly coat** with oil.
3. **Toss** with protein powder and seasonings in a big bowl.

Pro Tip

Flavored protein can get weird, but you might dig a sweet popcorn vibe. Experiment to find your sweet spot.

19. Seared Tofu Bites

Why It Rocks

High-protein tofu cubes, crisped up in a skillet with minimal effort. Perfect for vegetarians or anyone needing a meat-free option.

Ingredients

- 1 block extra-firm tofu, pressed
- 1 tbsp low-sodium soy sauce
- 1 tsp sesame oil (optional)
- Garlic powder, chili flakes

Method

1. **Cube** the tofu, pat dry.
2. **Marinate** briefly in soy sauce, sesame oil, and spices.
3. **Sear** in a hot pan until golden on all sides.

Pro Tip

Cook a batch and refrigerate. Munch on them cold or reheat for a quick protein fix—great with a dab of sriracha.

20. Meatless Meatballs

Why It Rocks
Plant-based "meatballs" are an easy, protein-boosting snack—just warm them up and dip in a little marinara.

Ingredients

- 1 bag frozen meatless meatballs (look for a brand high in protein, low in junk)
- Marinara sauce (low-sugar)

Method

1. **Heat** meatballs according to package instructions.
2. **Dip** in warmed marinara or serve on a small bed of zucchini noodles if you want more volume.

Pro Tip
Keep a bag in the freezer for emergencies. They're surprisingly versatile—throw 'em in soups, salads, or wraps.

Bottom Line

These **20** quick-fix snacks prove you don't need to resort to greasy junk or sugar-laden trash the second hunger strikes. They're **easy** to prep, taste damn good, and—most importantly—deliver the **protein** you need to keep your gains on track. Stock up, stash 'em everywhere, and show your cravings who's boss. Because around here, we don't **cave**; we **attack**.

CHAPTER 8: MEAL PREP LIKE A MANIAC— SAVING TIME WITHOUT GOING INSANE

Why settle for boring Sundays chained to the stove? Learn fast, organized meal prep strategies so you can kick back while the masses stress out.

Let's get one thing straight: **meal prep** shouldn't feel like a prison sentence. If your Sundays look like a never-ending slog of chopping, cooking, packing, and then collapsing on the couch, you're doing it wrong. **Why** settle for a day stolen by the stove when you can knock out your entire week's worth of meals in a fraction of the time—and still catch that Netflix binge, take a nap, or, hell, actually go out and live your life?

Here's the bottom line: **you either control your food**, or it controls you. If you're not prepping like a maniac—fast, focused, and efficient—then sooner or later you're gonna cave to the drive-thru, the vending machine, or the sad reality of microwaving some soggy mess at 9 p.m. while your gains slip through your fingers. The difference between people who *dominate* their diet and those who *complain* about never having time boils down to one word: **organization**. And that's exactly what this chapter is about—turning you into a meal-prep machine who breezes through the kitchen instead of being **chained** to it for hours.

Why Meal Prep Even Matters

Skip meal prep, and you'll be putting out fires all week long—scrambling for something half-edible and high in protein, or settling for greasy takeout that sets your macros on fire. It's a recipe for disaster (pun intended). On the flip side, if you take a little time to plan and prep, you'll have **ready-to-go meals** that keep you satisfied, fueled, and laser-focused on your lifts, your job, and, you know, real life. Think of meal prep as your **secret weapon** against chaos—it slashes stress, saves money, and stops you from rummaging through the freezer at 11 p.m. in a desperate hunt for pizza rolls.

Why Boring Sundays Are Overrated

Look, we've all heard the standard advice: "Just spend your Sunday cooking eight different dishes, and voila—done." But not everyone wants to blow their entire weekend stirring pots and washing mountains of Tupperware. This chapter will show you **smarter**, more streamlined ways to get it done. Whether you're using big-batch cooking, versatile base recipes, or clever shortcuts, the goal is to **save you time**, not rob you of your day off. Because guess what? You can still crush your macros **and** have a life.

Maniac-Level Strategies

We're not gonna give you some watered-down "cook once, eat forever" pitch that leaves you choking down the same bland chicken all week. Instead, we're talking **flexible** approaches—where you batch-cook key ingredients, swap flavors, and piece together meals like a pro. We'll dive into tips like:

- **Big-Batch Proteins**: Cook up a few pounds of chicken, lean beef, or tofu in one shot. Different seasonings, different sauces—new meals, zero extra headache.
- **Versatile Veggie Prep**: Chop your veggies in bulk, roast 'em, stir-fry 'em, or whatever you fancy. Then drop them into wraps, bowls, or side dishes all week without losing your mind.
- **One-Pot Wonders**: Master recipes that feed an army (or at least a week's worth of you) in a single pot or tray. Less cleanup, more gains.

Be a Control Freak (In a Good Way)

Meal prep is about **owning** your schedule. You decide when to shop, when to cook, and what goes into every meal. No more calling for last-minute pizza because you "didn't have anything in the fridge." No more drifting into the nearest fast-food line because you're too exhausted to brainstorm a healthy dinner. When your fridge is stocked with ready-to-eat, macro-friendly meals, you're in the driver's seat—and that's a damn good feeling.

Enjoy the Process or Speed Through It—Your Choice

Some people find the meal-prep ritual oddly therapeutic: chopping veggies, seasoning proteins, and stacking containers in the fridge like a badass. Others just want to get in, get out, and never look back. Either way, you do you. The point is, we'll show you how to do it **faster, easier**, and without losing your mind—or your entire Sunday. Because whether you're a culinary wizard or someone who can barely boil water without burning it, the strategies in this chapter are built to help you **keep it together** and come out on top.

Ready to Crush the Week?

So if you're tired of half-assing your diet just because you "don't have time," welcome to your wake-up call. You **can** meal-prep like a maniac without sacrificing your weekend, your wallet, or your sanity. And once you nail down these methods, you'll wonder how you ever managed without them. Let everyone else run around like headless chickens when Monday hits. You'll be sitting pretty, enjoying your perfectly portioned meals, and smiling at your next big PR in the gym.

It's time to **take control** and make meal prep work **for you**, not against you. Buckle up, because these next pages are your blueprint to ditch the culinary chaos and become the **ruthless** meal-prep master your future self will thank you for. Grab your containers, fire up your stove, and let's **get it done**—faster, smarter, and with a hell of a lot more flavor. Let's go.

Recipes Included: 10–15 bulk-cook basics (sheet-pan feasts, one-pot wonders, freezer-friendly staples)

Below are **15 bulk-cook basics**—the **mighty** recipes that help you crank out multiple servings in **one go**, so you can spend less time in the kitchen and more time dominating everything else. Each one is a **sheet-pan feast**, **one-pot wonder**, or **freezer-friendly** staple, keeping meal prep sane and your fridge stocked. Same format as always: **Why It Rocks**, **Ingredients**, **Method**, and a **Pro Tip**—so you can slam through your prep like a **true** meal-prep maniac.

1. One-Pan Chicken & Veggie Feast

Why It Rocks
No separate pans, minimal cleanup. You can bang out a week's worth of protein and veggies in a single shot—perfect for lunches or quick dinners.

Ingredients (Makes ~4–5 servings)

- 1½–2 lbs chicken breast or thighs (boneless, skinless)
- 3 cups chopped veggies (broccoli, carrots, zucchini)
- 2 tbsp olive oil
- Salt, pepper, and your favorite seasoning (Italian, Cajun, etc.)

Method

1. **Preheat** oven to 400°F (200°C).
2. **Toss** chicken and veggies with oil, salt, pepper, and seasonings on a sheet pan.
3. **Bake** ~20–25 minutes until chicken hits an internal temp of 165°F (74°C).

Pro Tip
Divide everything into containers as soon as it cools. Change up the seasoning each week (lemon pepper, taco seasoning, etc.) so you don't get bored.

2. Big-Batch Turkey Chili

Why It Rocks
A **one-pot** wonder: chili is hearty, freezer-friendly, and gets **better** the next day. Make a vat, freeze half, and you're set for weeks.

Ingredients (Makes ~6 servings)

- 1 lb lean ground turkey
- 1 onion, diced
- 1 bell pepper, diced
- 2 cans beans (kidney, black), drained
- 1 can (14–15 oz) diced tomatoes
- 2 tbsp chili powder, 1 tsp cumin, salt, pepper

Method

1. **Brown** turkey and onion in a large pot.
2. **Add** peppers, beans, tomatoes, and spices.
3. **Simmer** ~20–30 minutes, stirring occasionally.

Pro Tip
Portion out a couple servings for the fridge, then freeze the rest in individual containers. You'll thank yourself when you need a quick lunch next week.

3. Sheet-Pan Salmon & Root Veggies

Why It Rocks
Omega-3–rich salmon pairs with hearty root veggies (like sweet potatoes, carrots, parsnips) for a flavorful, **one-and-done** meal.

Ingredients (Makes ~3–4 servings)

- 1½ lbs salmon fillet (cut into portions)
- 3 cups chopped root veggies (sweet potatoes, carrots, beets)
- 2 tbsp olive oil
- Salt, pepper, herbs (rosemary, thyme)

Method

1. **Preheat** oven to 400°F (200°C).
2. **Coat** veggies with oil, salt, pepper, herbs; spread on sheet pan. Roast ~15 mins.
3. **Add** salmon on top or to one side, season. Roast another ~10–12 mins until salmon flakes.

Pro Tip
If you're meal-prepping, portion the salmon and veggies into containers. Add a lemon wedge if you want that fresh pop when you reheat.

4. Chicken, Brown Rice & Veggie Skillet

Why It Rocks
A **one-skillet** approach for a full meal—protein, carbs, veggies—done in one go, fewer dishes, more efficiency.

Ingredients (Makes ~4 servings)

- 1 lb chicken breast, cubed
- 1 onion, chopped
- 2 cups veggies (peas, carrots, peppers)
- 1 cup brown rice (dry)
- 2 cups chicken broth (low-sodium)
- Salt, pepper, garlic powder

Method

1. **Brown** chicken in a large skillet with onion; season with salt, pepper, garlic.
2. **Add** rice, broth, and veggies.
3. **Cover** and simmer ~20–25 minutes until rice is tender.

Pro Tip
Want some extra flavor? Splash in a bit of soy sauce, teriyaki, or your favorite spices. This base recipe is easy to twist any way you want.

5. Beef & Barley Soup (Freezer-Friendly)

Why It Rocks
Thick, hearty soup that's simple to portion out and freeze. Barley boosts carbs/fiber, beef brings the protein.

Ingredients (Makes ~6 servings)

- 1 lb lean stewing beef
- 1 onion, chopped
- 2 carrots, sliced
- 2 celery stalks, sliced
- ½ cup pearl barley
- 4–5 cups beef broth (low-sodium)
- Salt, pepper, thyme

Method

1. **Brown** beef in a large pot; add onion, carrots, celery.
2. **Toss** in barley and broth, along with thyme, salt, pepper.
3. **Simmer** ~40–45 minutes until beef is tender and barley is cooked.

Pro Tip

Cool, portion into freezer-friendly containers. Reheat whenever you need a cozy, protein-loaded meal without the hassle.

6. Tofu & Veggie Stir-Fry (with Bulk Sauce)

Why It Rocks
Stir-fries are your friend: quick, versatile, and great for a **big batch**. The secret is prepping a **bulk stir-fry sauce** you can use all week.

Ingredients (Makes ~4 servings)

- 1 block firm tofu, drained & cubed
- 4 cups mixed veggies (broccoli, carrots, peppers)
- 1 tbsp oil (sesame or olive)
- Bulk sauce: ½ cup low-sodium soy sauce, 2 tbsp cornstarch, 2 tbsp water, 2 tbsp honey (optional), garlic, ginger

Method

1. **Sear** tofu in oil until golden. Remove.
2. **Stir-fry** veggies.
3. **Combine** sauce ingredients in a jar—shake well.
4. **Return** tofu to pan, pour in sauce, let it thicken.

Pro Tip
Double the sauce and store in the fridge. Next time you make chicken or shrimp, you've already got a stir-fry sauce ready to go.

7. Big-Batch Egg Muffins

Why It Rocks
Breakfast (or snack) prepped in muffin form—easy to cook in bulk, keep in the fridge or freezer, then reheat on demand.

Ingredients (Makes ~12 muffins)

- 10–12 eggs (or a mix of whole eggs + egg whites)
- 1 cup chopped veggies (spinach, bell peppers, onions)
- Salt, pepper, any other seasoning
- Optional: diced turkey bacon or low-fat cheese

Method

1. **Preheat** oven to 350°F (175°C). Spray a muffin tin.
2. **Whisk** eggs, add veggies and optional items. Season.
3. **Pour** mixture into muffin cups ~¾ full.
4. **Bake** ~15–20 minutes until set.

Pro Tip
Let them cool before popping them out. Store in containers for up to a week, or freeze for a month. Quick protein fix, zero excuses.

8. Crockpot Chicken Tacos

Why It Rocks
Dump everything in a **slow cooker**, come back to flavorful, shredded chicken perfect for tacos, salads, or bowls.

Ingredients (Makes ~6 servings)

- 2–3 lbs chicken breasts
- 1 can diced tomatoes (14–15 oz)
- 1 packet (or homemade) taco seasoning
- 1 onion, sliced (optional)

Method

1. **Place** chicken, tomatoes, seasoning, onion in crockpot.
2. **Cook** on low ~6–7 hours (or high ~3–4).
3. **Shred** chicken with forks.

Pro Tip
Use the shredded chicken in tacos, burritos, salads—whatever. Freeze any extra in portioned bags so you're always ready to rock.

9. Sheet-Pan Steak & Veggies

Why It Rocks

One-pan steak dinner without the fuss, perfect for slicing and portioning into meal-prep containers.

Ingredients (Makes ~4 servings)

- 1½–2 lbs lean steak (sirloin, flank)
- 2 cups chopped veggies (bell peppers, onions, zucchini)
- 2 tbsp olive oil
- Salt, pepper, steak seasoning blend

Method

1. **Preheat** oven to 425°F (220°C).
2. **Toss** veggies with oil, salt, pepper. Spread on sheet pan.
3. **Season** steak, place on pan.
4. **Roast** ~10–12 minutes (depending on desired doneness).

Pro Tip

Let steak rest 5 minutes, slice thinly. Serve over brown rice or potatoes if you need carbs, or keep it low-carb with extra veggies.

10. One-Pot Lentil & Veggie Soup

Why It Rocks

Hearty, high in fiber and plant-based protein. Lentils cook relatively fast, so you can churn out a big pot in under an hour.

Ingredients (Makes ~6 servings)

- 1 cup dried lentils, rinsed
- 1 onion, diced
- 2 carrots, diced
- 2 celery stalks, diced
- 4–5 cups vegetable broth
- Salt, pepper, Italian herbs

Method

1. **Sauté** onion, carrots, celery in a pot.
2. **Add** lentils, broth, herbs, salt, pepper.

3. **Simmer** ~20–25 minutes until lentils are tender.

Pro Tip
Freeze half if you're cooking for one or two. Lentil soup rethaws like a dream, so you can have a hot meal in minutes.

11. Roasted Chicken Breasts with Sweet Potatoes

Why It Rocks
Another simple sheet-pan approach. Cook chicken and sweet potatoes together, toss in some greens near the end—done.

Ingredients (Makes ~3–4 servings)

- 1½ lbs chicken breasts
- 2 sweet potatoes, cut into chunks
- 1 tbsp olive oil
- Salt, pepper, paprika

Method

1. **Preheat** oven to 400°F (200°C).
2. **Toss** sweet potato chunks with oil, paprika, salt, pepper on sheet pan. Roast ~10 mins first.
3. **Add** chicken breasts, season them. Roast another ~20 mins until chicken is cooked.

Pro Tip
Swap sweet potatoes for regular potatoes or a mix of veggies if you need more variety. This is a prep staple that's impossible to screw up.

12. Big-Batch Quinoa & Veggies

Why It Rocks
Make a **huge** pot of quinoa, roast a bunch of veggies, combine, and you've got a flexible base for the entire week. Perfect for bowls, salads, or sides.

Ingredients (Makes ~4–5 servings)

- 2 cups quinoa (dry)
- 4 cups water or broth
- 4 cups assorted veggies (bell peppers, zucchini, onions, mushrooms)
- 2 tbsp olive oil

- Salt, pepper, herbs (oregano, basil, etc.)

Method

1. **Cook** quinoa according to package (usually 1 part quinoa to 2 parts liquid, ~15–20 mins).
2. **Chop** veggies, toss in oil, season. Roast at 400°F (200°C) ~15–20 mins.
3. **Combine** cooked quinoa and roasted veggies in a big bowl.

Pro Tip

Mix in a light dressing (balsamic, lemon-garlic, etc.) to keep it fresh. Store in separate containers or all together, depending on how you plan to use it.

13. Turkey & Brown Rice Casserole

Why It Rocks

A simple casserole that's easy to portion out and reheat. Turkey + brown rice + veggies + light sauce = balanced macros.

Ingredients (Makes ~4–5 servings)

- 1 lb ground turkey
- 1 onion, diced
- 3 cups cooked brown rice
- 2 cups chopped veggies (broccoli florets, carrots)
- 1 cup low-fat soup or sauce (e.g., cream of mushroom, cream of chicken—low-sodium if possible)
- Salt, pepper

Method

1. **Brown** turkey and onion in a skillet.
2. **Combine** cooked rice, turkey, veggies, soup in a casserole dish.
3. **Bake** at 375°F (190°C) ~20–25 mins until hot and bubbling.

Pro Tip

Sprinkle on a little low-fat cheese in the last 5 minutes if you want a cheesy crust without drowning in calories.

14. Slow-Cooker Pulled Pork

Why It Rocks
Make a giant batch of lean pulled pork, use it in sandwiches, tacos, or bowls all week. Freeze extra if you've got leftovers.

Ingredients (Makes ~6 servings)

- 2–3 lbs pork loin (trimmed)
- 1 cup low-sugar BBQ sauce or simple seasoning + broth
- 1 onion, sliced (optional)

Method

1. **Place** pork and onion in slow cooker.
2. **Add** BBQ sauce (or broth + seasoning).
3. **Cook** on low ~7–8 hours.
4. **Shred** pork with forks.

Pro Tip
Check the sauce label for sugar content. If it's too high, cut it with water or use a sugar-free variant to keep macros in check.

15. Bulk Meatballs (Freeze for Later)

Why It Rocks
Meatballs are versatile. Make 'em in bulk with lean beef or turkey, freeze the extras, and you've got instant protein whenever you need it.

Ingredients (Makes ~20–24 meatballs)

- 1½ lbs lean ground beef or turkey
- 1 egg
- ½ cup breadcrumbs (whole-wheat if possible)
- Salt, pepper, Italian seasoning
- Optional: grated onion, garlic powder

Method

1. **Preheat** oven to 400°F (200°C).
2. **Mix** meat, egg, breadcrumbs, and seasonings in a bowl.
3. **Form** meatballs, place on baking sheet.

4. **Bake** ~15–20 minutes or until internal temp hits 160°F (71°C) for beef or 165°F (74°C) for turkey.

Pro Tip
Cool, freeze in a single layer on a sheet pan, then transfer to a bag. That way, they don't stick together, and you can thaw as many as you want at a time.

Final Word

These **15 bulk-cook** recipes are your ticket to **fast, organized** meal prep—each one is easy to scale up or down, **freezer-friendly**, and designed to cut your cook time in half without sacrificing taste. Line up a couple of these each weekend, and you'll stomp out the excuses faster than you can say "drive-thru." **Cook like a maniac**, stock your fridge, and reclaim your week—because you've got bigger fish to fry than scrambling for meals every day.

CHAPTER 9: FLAVOR OVERDRIVE—SAUCES, SPICES, AND SEASONINGS THAT SLAP

Bump your meals from meh to hell yeah with these simple but powerful flavor hacks. Because nobody wants to live on plain chicken forever.

Listen, no one's out here trying to eat dull, flavorless meals day after day. Unless you're a masochist—or you've got a thing for bland chicken breasts—odds are you need some **serious flavor** to keep your taste buds from tapping out. This chapter is your secret weapon: a stash of **simple but powerful** hacks for revving up your protein, veggies, and even your go-to carbs. Because, let's face it, you can have the best macros on the planet—but if your meals taste like cardboard, you're flirting with a diet meltdown in record time.

Why Flavor Matters More Than You Think

If you're forcing down boring food, you'll eventually crack. That's a one-way ticket to random snack binges and fast-food cheat-fests. On the flip side, if you know how to **season like a pro**—tossing in the right spices, marinades, or sauces—you'll actually *look forward* to your meals. Translation: you stick to your plan, crush your macros, and keep your sanity intact. Call it **culinary self-defense**—a must-have if you want long-term success.

Give Plain Chicken (and Everything Else) a Break

Chicken, fish, tofu—whatever protein you're rocking—**doesn't** have to be a snoozefest. All it needs is the right rub, marinade, or sauce, and suddenly you've gone from zero to "holy hell, that's good!" in under ten minutes. Same goes for veggies. Coat a pan of broccoli florets in a **fiery chipotle rub**, or toss zucchini with a **lemon-garlic marinade**. The difference is staggering, and it's all in **how** you season.

No Fancy Ingredients Required

Don't panic if your spice cabinet looks like a sad salt-and-pepper wasteland. We'll show you **key staples**—like smoked paprika, garlic powder, onion powder, chili flakes, dried herbs—that explode with flavor without costing a fortune or requiring some specialty gourmet trip. Whether you're a kitchen newbie or a seasoned (ha!) chef, these flavor boosters are easy to sprinkle, rub, whisk, or brush onto just about anything you cook.

Keep It Interesting

Think of your meals as a base—chicken breast, tofu, eggs, salmon, or a tray of roasted veggies. Now, multiply those by unlimited flavor combos. A **simple marinade** here, a **bold rub** there, a **tangy sauce** on top—voilà, your rotation just got exponentially bigger. Say goodbye to the monotony that makes you want to throw in the towel by midweek. With a well-stocked spice rack and a few **killer sauces**, you can dial up the variety without reinventing the wheel every time.

Ready to Crank It Up?

This chapter isn't about any rigid formula; it's about *empowering* you to take whatever you're cooking and **launch** it into Flavor Overdrive. We'll cover **basic rubs**, **oil-free marinades**, **low-sugar sauces**, and **herb mixes** you can whip up in seconds. Don't be surprised if your once-boring meal prep suddenly turns into a highlight of your day. When your food hits that "damn, that's good" level, sticking to your plan is a breeze.

So buckle up. It's time to shelve the bland nonsense and load up on **spices, sauces, and seasonings** that'll make your taste buds go wild—without blowing your macros. Let's take your meals from **meh** to **hell yeah** in no time flat. Because life's too short for boring-ass chicken, right? Let's do this.

Recipes Included: 15–20 sauce and seasoning combos to turbocharge any dish

Below are **20** sauce-and-seasoning combos that pack a **massive** flavor punch without derailing your macros. Each one follows the familiar format—**Why It Rocks**, **Ingredients**, **Method**, and a **Pro Tip**—so you can whip them up in seconds and **turbocharge** your chicken, fish, tofu, veggies, or whatever else needs a good kick in the taste buds.

1. Hot & Smoky Chipotle Rub

Why It Rocks
Perfect for grilled chicken, fish, tofu, or even roasted veggies—adds bold flavor with minimal calories.

Ingredients (Makes ~1 cup of rub)

- 2 tbsp chipotle powder
- 2 tbsp smoked paprika
- 1 tbsp garlic powder
- 1 tbsp onion powder

- 1 tsp cayenne pepper (or less if you're not a heat freak)
- 1 tbsp salt
- 1 tbsp ground black pepper

Method

1. **Combine** all the spices in a small bowl or jar.
2. **Stir** or **shake** well until evenly mixed.
3. **Store** in an airtight container for up to 3 months.

Pro Tip

Rub it generously onto proteins (or veggies) about 15–30 minutes before cooking. Let the flavors sink in—then grill, bake, or sauté to let the heat and smoke do their thing.

2. Zesty Lemon-Garlic Marinade

Why It Rocks

Bright, tangy, and a total game-changer for bland chicken or fish. Citrus and garlic = instant flavor boost.

Ingredients (Enough for ~1–1.5 lbs of protein)

- ¼ cup freshly squeezed lemon juice
- 2 tbsp olive oil (divide across multiple servings = minimal extra fat)
- 3 cloves garlic, minced (or 1 tbsp garlic paste)
- 1 tsp dried oregano
- ½ tsp salt
- ¼ tsp black pepper

Method

1. **Whisk** all ingredients in a small bowl.
2. **Marinate** your protein (chicken breasts, fish fillets, tofu, etc.) at least 30 minutes, up to 2 hours.
3. **Grill, bake, or pan-sear** as you like.

Pro Tip

Don't marinate delicate fish too long or it'll go mushy. For chicken, overnight in the fridge = flavor city.

3. Sweet & Spicy Sriracha Honey Glaze

Why It Rocks
Sticky, spicy, and downright addictive. Perfect for brushing onto chicken thighs or coating roasted veggies.

Ingredients (Makes ~¾ cup)

- ¼ cup honey
- 2 tbsp sriracha (or more if you're a spice fiend)
- 1 tbsp soy sauce
- 1 tbsp rice vinegar
- 1 clove garlic, grated (optional)

Method

1. **Whisk** all ingredients in a small bowl.
2. **Brush** onto protein or veggies in the last 5 minutes of cooking, or toss everything in a bowl after it's cooked.

Pro Tip
If you want a thicker glaze, simmer everything for a few minutes on the stove until it reduces. Boom—instant sticky goodness.

4. Classic Herb Rub

Why It Rocks
Simple but versatile. Works on just about everything—chicken, fish, steak, roasted veggies. Think "Italian seasoning on steroids."

Ingredients (Makes ~½ cup)

- 2 tbsp dried basil
- 2 tbsp dried oregano
- 2 tbsp dried thyme
- 1 tbsp dried rosemary
- 1 tbsp garlic powder
- 1 tsp salt
- 1 tsp black pepper

Method

1. **Mix** all herbs and spices in a small jar.

2. **Shake** until well combined.
3. **Use** as a dry rub before grilling or roasting.

Pro Tip

Combine with a bit of olive oil or lemon juice to make a quick marinade paste. That'll help the herbs stick and penetrate your protein.

5. Creamy Greek Yogurt Sauce

Why It Rocks

High-protein alternative to mayo or sour cream. Great as a drizzle on wraps, a dip for veggies, or a topping for grilled chicken.

Ingredients (Makes ~1 cup)

- 1 cup plain Greek yogurt
- 1 clove garlic, minced
- Juice of ½ lemon
- ½ tsp salt
- ¼ tsp pepper
- Optional herbs: dill, parsley, basil

Method

1. **Combine** everything in a bowl.
2. **Stir** until smooth.
3. **Chill** at least 15 minutes to let flavors meld.

Pro Tip

Elevate it: add chopped cucumber (for tzatziki vibes) or a dash of sriracha if you want heat.

6. DIY Taco Seasoning

Why It Rocks

No mystery fillers or insane sodium. Control the spice level yourself, and skip the store-bought packets full of junk.

Ingredients (Makes ~¼ cup)

- 1 tbsp chili powder
- 1 tsp cumin

- 1 tsp paprika
- 1 tsp garlic powder
- 1 tsp onion powder
- ½ tsp dried oregano
- ½ tsp salt (or more to taste)
- ¼ tsp black pepper
- Optional: pinch of cayenne

Method

1. **Mix** everything in a small jar.
2. **Use** ~1–2 tbsp per pound of ground meat or veggie alternative.

Pro Tip
Adjust salt and cayenne to suit your dietary needs and heat tolerance. No more bland tacos—ever.

7. Asian-Inspired Teriyaki Sauce

Why It Rocks
Sticky, sweet, and perfect for stir-fries or glazing salmon. Store-bought versions can be sugar bombs—make your own with better control.

Ingredients (Makes ~1 cup)

- ½ cup low-sodium soy sauce
- ¼ cup water
- 2 tbsp honey (or maple syrup)
- 1 tbsp rice vinegar
- 1 tsp minced fresh ginger (or ½ tsp dried)
- 1 clove garlic, minced
- 1 tsp cornstarch + 1 tbsp water (slurry)
- Pinch of chili flakes (optional)

Method

1. **Combine** soy sauce, water, honey, vinegar, garlic, ginger, chili flakes in a saucepan.
2. **Bring** to a simmer over medium heat.
3. **Stir** in cornstarch slurry; keep stirring until thickened (~1–2 mins).
4. **Remove** from heat.

Pro Tip
Baste salmon or chicken thighs in the last minutes of cooking, or use as a stir-fry sauce. Reserve a bit on the side for dipping—but don't use raw marinade as sauce.

8. Spice Jerk Rub

Why It Rocks
Caribbean-inspired heat with a sweet-savory punch. Ideal for chicken thighs, shrimp, or even tofu steaks.

Ingredients (Makes ~½ cup)

- 1 tbsp allspice
- 1 tbsp dried thyme
- 2 tsp cayenne (adjust heat if you're a mortal)
- 1 tbsp brown sugar (optional)
- 1 tsp cinnamon
- 1 tsp nutmeg
- 1 tbsp garlic powder
- 1 tsp salt
- ½ tsp black pepper

Method

1. **Stir** all spices in a bowl.
2. **Rub** onto protein; marinate if possible to deepen flavor.

Pro Tip
Amp up authenticity by adding a dash of lime juice and fresh chili peppers (like Scotch bonnet) if you dare.

9. Roasted Garlic & Herb Butter (Lightened Up)

Why It Rocks
Butter can add crazy flavor—but it can also destroy macros if you're not careful. Go half-and-half with Greek yogurt for a lighter spread.

Ingredients (Makes ~½ cup)

- 2 tbsp softened butter
- 2 tbsp Greek yogurt

- 2 cloves roasted garlic, mashed
- ½ tsp dried thyme
- ½ tsp dried rosemary
- Pinch of salt, pepper

Method

1. **Combine** butter and yogurt until smooth.
2. **Mix** in roasted garlic and herbs.
3. **Store** in the fridge, use sparingly.

Pro Tip

Spread on crusty whole-grain bread or melt a bit over steamed veggies for a flavor bomb that won't wreck your macros.

10. Citrus-Chili Marinade

Why It Rocks

Bright citrus zing + a spicy kick = perfect for chicken breast, shrimp, or even pork tenderloin. Great for summer grilling.

Ingredients (Enough for ~1–1.5 lbs protein)

- Juice of 1 orange + 1 lime
- 1 tbsp olive oil
- 1 tsp chili powder
- 1 clove garlic, minced
- ½ tsp salt
- ¼ tsp pepper

Method

1. **Whisk** all ingredients in a bowl.
2. **Marinate** protein for at least 30 mins (up to 2 hours).
3. **Grill or bake**, savor that tangy heat.

Pro Tip

Save a little marinade on the side (unused) to drizzle over the cooked protein—just be sure to keep raw marinade separate.

11. All-Purpose Seasoning Blend

Why It Rocks
One jar to rule them all. Salt, pepper, garlic, onion, paprika—boom. Shake it on anything that needs a flavor bump.

Ingredients (Makes ~¼ cup)

- 1 tbsp salt
- 1 tbsp black pepper
- 1 tbsp garlic powder
- 1 tbsp onion powder
- 1 tbsp paprika

Method

1. **Combine** everything in a small container.
2. **Sprinkle** on chicken, veggies, fries—whatever.

Pro Tip
Keep a shaker of this by the stove. Whenever a dish tastes a little flat, toss some in.

12. Low-Sugar BBQ Sauce

Why It Rocks
Commercial BBQ sauces often come with insane sugar counts. This version cuts it down while staying smoky and tangy.

Ingredients (Makes ~1 cup)

- 1 cup tomato sauce (no salt/sugar added if possible)
- 2 tbsp apple cider vinegar
- 1 tbsp Worcestershire sauce
- 1 tbsp honey (or maple syrup)
- 1 tsp smoked paprika
- 1 clove garlic, minced
- Salt, pepper to taste

Method

1. **Whisk** all ingredients in a small saucepan.
2. **Simmer** on low ~5–10 mins for flavors to meld.

Pro Tip

Taste and adjust sweetness or smokiness as needed. Make a big batch and store in the fridge for weeks of BBQ bliss.

13. Peanut-Lime Stir-Fry Sauce

Why It Rocks

Creamy, tangy, and perfect for tossing with noodles, veggies, or chicken in a stir-fry. Also works as a dipping sauce.

Ingredients (Makes ~½ cup)

- 2 tbsp peanut butter (natural)
- 2 tbsp soy sauce (low-sodium)
- 1 tbsp lime juice
- 1 tsp honey (optional)
- 1 tsp grated ginger or ½ tsp ginger powder
- Pinch of chili flakes (if you want heat)

Method

1. **Whisk** all ingredients in a bowl.
2. **Thin** with water if needed for consistency.

Pro Tip

Serve over warm dishes so the sauce melts into everything. You can also add a touch of coconut milk if you're feeling indulgent.

14. Chili-Lime Dry Rub

Why It Rocks

Great for those who want flavor minus the extra sauce. Chili powder and lime zest bring tangy heat to any protein.

Ingredients (Makes ~¼ cup)

- 2 tbsp chili powder
- Zest of 1 lime (dried in the oven if possible)
- 1 tbsp cumin
- 1 tsp salt
- 1 tsp black pepper

- 1 tsp garlic powder

Method

1. **Mix** all ingredients in a small bowl.
2. **Rub** onto protein—chicken, shrimp, fish—before grilling or baking.

Pro Tip
If you don't want to fuss with drying lime zest, just add fresh zest right before cooking for a burst of tang.

15. Garlicky Yogurt Ranch

Why It Rocks
Ranch cravings are real—but typical ranch dressing can be a calorie nightmare. This Greek yogurt version slashes fat and ups protein.

Ingredients (Makes ~1 cup)

- 1 cup Greek yogurt
- 1 tsp dried dill
- ½ tsp onion powder
- ½ tsp garlic powder
- ½ tsp salt
- ¼ tsp black pepper
- Splash of milk (low-fat or almond) to thin

Method

1. **Combine** yogurt and seasonings in a bowl.
2. **Stir**, add milk until desired consistency.

Pro Tip
Use as a dip for veggies, a drizzle for wraps, or even thin it more for a salad dressing. Way better than store-bought ranch bombs.

16. Buffalo Marinade

Why It Rocks
Spicy, vinegary kick for your chicken or cauliflower "wings." Especially good if you're craving Buffalo sauce but want it less buttery.

Ingredients (Makes enough for ~1 lb protein)

- ¼ cup hot sauce (Frank's RedHot is classic)
- 2 tbsp white vinegar
- 1 tbsp olive oil
- 1 tsp garlic powder
- 1 tsp onion powder
- Pinch of salt

Method

1. **Whisk** all ingredients.
2. **Marinate** your chicken or cauliflower florets ~30 mins.
3. **Bake**, grill, or air-fry.

Pro Tip

After cooking, toss with a bit more hot sauce (or a dab of melted light butter) for a true Buffalo finish.

17. Ginger-Garlic Spice Rub

Why It Rocks

Warm ginger notes and garlicky goodness—fantastic for Asian-inspired dishes or when you want a break from standard herb rubs.

Ingredients (Makes ~¼ cup)

- 1 tbsp ground ginger
- 1 tbsp garlic powder
- 1 tbsp onion powder
- 1 tsp salt
- 1 tsp black pepper
- 1 tsp chili flakes (optional)

Method

1. **Stir** all spices.
2. **Rub** onto chicken, pork, or tofu before cooking.

Pro Tip

Pair with a drizzle of soy sauce or teriyaki post-cooking for next-level umami.

18. Tomato-Basil Pesto (Lightened)

Why It Rocks
Traditional pesto is heavy on oil and cheese. This version uses more basil, tomato, and a bit less oil—still tastes amazing over pasta or chicken.

Ingredients (Makes ~1 cup)

- 2 cups fresh basil
- ½ cup sundried tomatoes (drained if in oil)
- 2 tbsp pine nuts (or walnuts)
- 1 tbsp olive oil
- 2 tbsp water (to thin)
- 1 clove garlic
- Salt, pepper to taste

Method

1. **Blend** all ingredients in a food processor, scraping sides as needed.
2. **Add** more water or oil if necessary to achieve desired consistency.

Pro Tip
Toss with spiralized veggies, whole-wheat pasta, or smear on sandwiches for a killer flavor punch.

19. Lemon Pepper Seasoning

Why It Rocks
A bright, tangy seasoning that wakes up chicken, fish, or even veggies. Store-bought can be loaded with fillers; homemade is simpler and cleaner.

Ingredients (Makes ~¼ cup)

- Zest of 2 lemons (dried, if possible)
- 1 tbsp black pepper
- 1 tsp onion powder
- 1 tsp garlic powder
- 1 tsp salt

Method

1. **Mix** all ingredients in a small jar.
2. **Sprinkle** on your protein or veggies before cooking.

Pro Tip

To dry lemon zest, spread it on a baking sheet at the lowest oven temp for ~15 minutes. Store in an airtight container.

20. Smoky Chipotle Salsa

Why It Rocks

A fresh salsa with a chipotle twist—fantastic on tacos, grilled chicken, or as a dip. Minimal calories, max flavor.

Ingredients (Makes ~2 cups)

- 1 can (14–15 oz) diced tomatoes (fire-roasted if you can)
- 1 chipotle pepper in adobo sauce (or more if you like heat)
- ¼ onion, chopped
- 1 clove garlic, minced
- Juice of ½ lime
- Salt, pepper to taste

Method

1. **Blend** everything in a food processor or blender to desired chunkiness.
2. **Taste** and adjust salt/lime/heat.

Pro Tip

Use leftover salsa to spice up scrambled eggs, grilled fish, or even stir it into soup for a smoky kick.

Final Word

With these **20 sauce and seasoning combos**, you've got an **arsenal** of flavor weapons to unleash on anything you cook—without torpedoing your macros. Swap them in, mix them up, and **never** settle for plain, boring meals again. Because a diet that tastes awesome is the one you'll actually **stick to**—and that's how you stay winning. Go forth, flavor warrior, and turn every dish into a **culinary knockout**.

CHAPTER 10: CHEAT MEALS THAT WON'T WRECK YOUR GAINS

Yes, you can cheat without blowing up your progress. Here's how—just don't turn a cheat meal into a cheat week if you want to keep crushing goals.

Let's drop the guilt trip: **cheat meals** are a real thing, and pretending you'll never crave a cheesy slice of pizza or a stack of syrup-drenched waffles is just naïve. The good news? You can absolutely **indulge** without detonating your hard-earned progress—*if* you play your cards right. This chapter is your crash course in **cheating responsibly**. Because there's a big difference between enjoying a well-planned cheat meal and turning your entire week into a festival of junk that sets you back to square one.

Why Cheat Meals Matter (and Why They Don't Have to Ruin You)

Think of cheat meals as a **pressure release valve**. Stick to a rigid plan 24/7 without a single taste of the "forbidden," and you risk snapping from the built-up tension. Eventually, you might cave in a spectacular fashion, demolishing an entire pizza or burying your sorrows in a tub of ice cream—**and** regret. A smart cheat meal, on the other hand, can help you **stay sane**, satisfy cravings, and jump back on track with minimal damage.

Cheat Meal vs. Cheat Week—There's a Difference

A cheat meal can be a tactical break from your usual diet—one meal, or maybe a dessert—where you loosen the reins. But if you let that meal bleed into leftovers for the next day, grab a donut for breakfast "because why not," then decide to celebrate Taco Tuesday with an all-day food fest, you've crossed the line into cheat **week** territory. That's how you bury your gains. The trick is to **plan** your indulgence, enjoy it to the fullest, and then **stop**—returning to your regularly scheduled macros without skipping a beat.

Don't Let "Cheat" Become "Self-Destruct"

Eating a burger and fries doesn't have to spiral into a meltdown of guilt or a gateway to devouring a family-sized bag of chips before bedtime. The key is **mindful cheating**: you own your choice, you relish every bite, and then you move on. No shame, no hand-wringing, no "well, I already messed up, so let's keep going." That mindset will take you from a manageable blip to a multi-day disaster. Instead, let your cheat meal be a short, sweet detour—not a destructive rampage.

Ready to Cheat Without Hating Yourself Later?

This chapter will show you exactly how to **pick** the right cheat foods, **time** them for maximum enjoyment (and minimal damage), and **balance** your macros around them so you don't nuke your weekly progress. Because let's be real: life is too short not to enjoy a slice of pizza once in a while. The goal is to do it **intelligently**, so you can have your cheat and keep crushing those goals, too. Flip the page, and let's dive into the art of the strategic cheat meal—where taste buds and gains can coexist peacefully. No regrets, no excuses, just smart indulgence. Let's go.

Recipes Included: 15 indulgent-but-smart cheat ideas (high-protein pizza, guilt-free desserts)

Below are **15** cheat-meal ideas that let you **indulge** without sending your progress straight to hell. Each one follows our usual format—**Why It Rocks**, **Ingredients**, **Method**, and a **Pro Tip**—so you can whip them up and **savor** every bite. They're still "cheats," but with a **smarter** macro twist—because you don't have to wreck your gains just to treat yourself.

1. High-Protein Pepperoni Pizza

Why It Rocks
Because pizza cravings are real, and store-bought pies can nuke your macros. This version cuts down on carbs/fat while **jacking up** the protein—so you can crush that pizza itch without feeling like you bombed your diet.

Ingredients (Makes 1 medium pizza)

- 1 high-protein or whole-wheat pizza crust (store-bought or homemade)
- ½ cup tomato sauce (low-sugar if possible)
- 1 cup low-fat mozzarella cheese, shredded
- 12–15 slices turkey pepperoni
- Optional add-ons: veggies (bell peppers, onions, mushrooms)

Method

1. **Preheat** oven to crust instructions (usually ~425°F/220°C).
2. **Spread** sauce over the crust, sprinkle cheese, arrange pepperoni.
3. **Bake** ~10–12 minutes until cheese melts and crust is crispy.

Pro Tip
Swap out pepperoni for grilled chicken or lean ground turkey if you want even more protein. You can also add extra veggies for flavor and fiber.

2. Protein-Loaded Cheeseburger

Why It Rocks
Sometimes you just want a **big, juicy burger**. Using lean beef (or bison/turkey), a lighter bun, and strategic toppings keeps it cheat-ish without the fat bomb.

Ingredients (Makes 1 burger)

- 6 oz lean ground beef (90% lean or better)
- 1 whole-wheat bun (or low-cal bun)
- 1 slice reduced-fat cheese
- Lettuce, tomato, onion, pickles
- Ketchup, mustard, or light mayo (in moderation)

Method

1. **Form** beef into a patty, season with salt, pepper, maybe a dash of Worcestershire sauce.
2. **Grill or pan-sear** until cooked to preferred doneness.
3. **Assemble** on the bun with cheese, veggies, and condiments.

Pro Tip
Go easy on the sauces—they can skyrocket calories. Pair your burger with baked sweet potato fries or a side salad to keep it from turning into a full-blown calorie fest.

3. Guilt-Free Mac & Cheese

Why It Rocks
Creamy comfort food that doesn't punch your macros in the face. A mix of lighter cheese, Greek yogurt, and whole-wheat or high-protein pasta gets the job done.

Ingredients (Serves ~2)

- 2 cups whole-wheat or chickpea pasta
- 1 cup low-fat shredded cheddar (or a blend)
- ¼ cup plain Greek yogurt
- ¼ cup low-fat milk (adjust to desired creaminess)
- Salt, pepper, pinch of garlic powder

Method

1. **Cook** pasta per package directions; drain.
2. **Return** to pot; stir in cheese, yogurt, milk, and seasonings.
3. **Heat** on low until cheese melts and it's nice and creamy.

Pro Tip

Add diced chicken or tuna for extra protein. You can also toss in steamed broccoli to up the fiber and keep you feeling full.

4. Oven-"Fried" Chicken Tenders

Why It Rocks

Crunchy, savory chicken with a fraction of the oil. Using panko or whole-wheat breadcrumbs and baking instead of frying cuts the guilt but not the flavor.

Ingredients (~2 servings)

- 1 lb chicken tenders (or sliced chicken breast)
- 1 cup whole-wheat breadcrumbs or panko
- 1 egg + 1 egg white, beaten
- Seasonings: salt, pepper, paprika, garlic powder

Method

1. **Preheat** oven to 400°F (200°C). Line a baking sheet with foil or parchment.
2. **Dip** tenders in beaten egg, then coat in breadcrumbs mixed with seasonings.
3. **Arrange** on sheet; bake ~15–20 minutes until crispy and cooked through.

Pro Tip

Serve with a homemade low-sugar BBQ sauce or Greek yogurt ranch for dipping—satisfies that fast-food craving without the oil slick.

5. Protein Cheesecake Cups

Why It Rocks

Cheesecake that feeds your sweet tooth *and* your muscles. Using Greek yogurt, reduced-fat cream cheese, and a scoop of protein powder = dessert that doesn't nuke your progress.

Ingredients (Makes ~6 cups)

- 8 oz reduced-fat cream cheese, softened
- 1 cup plain Greek yogurt
- 1 scoop vanilla protein powder
- ¼ cup sweetener (stevia, monk fruit, or a bit of sugar—your call)
- 1 egg
- 1 tsp vanilla extract

Method

1. **Preheat** oven to 325°F (160°C). Line a muffin tin with paper liners.
2. **Blend** all ingredients until smooth.
3. **Pour** into liners and bake ~15–20 minutes until set.
4. **Chill** in fridge for at least an hour before serving.

Pro Tip

Top with fresh berries or a drizzle of sugar-free syrup. Instant fancy dessert that won't weigh you down.

6. Pizzadillas (Pizza Quesadillas)

Why It Rocks

When you can't decide between pizza or quesadillas, have both. A lighter tortilla, some sauce, cheese, and your protein of choice keep it (sort of) cheat-ish yet balanced.

Ingredients (Makes 1 pizzadilla)

- 1 whole-wheat tortilla
- 2–3 tbsp tomato sauce
- ¼ cup low-fat mozzarella
- Toppings: turkey pepperoni, lean ground beef, veggies

Method

1. **Spread** sauce on tortilla, sprinkle cheese, add toppings.
2. **Fold** in half. Cook in a skillet over medium heat ~2–3 mins each side until cheese melts.

Pro Tip

Cut into wedges, serve with a side salad for extra volume. Switch up the fillings (chicken, mushrooms, etc.) to keep it interesting.

7. Protein Ice Cream (Banana Soft-Serve)

Why It Rocks

Creamy, sweet, and can easily boost the protein. Made from frozen bananas + your choice of add-ins. Tastes like soft-serve, minus the insane sugar.

Ingredients (~2 servings)

- 2 ripe bananas, frozen (peeled, sliced)
- 1 scoop vanilla or chocolate protein powder
- Splash of almond milk (if needed)
- Optional: peanut butter, cocoa powder

Method

1. **Blend** frozen bananas and protein in a food processor.
2. **Add** milk if it's too thick.
3. **Scoop** into a bowl, enjoy immediately (soft-serve style).

Pro Tip

Sprinkle with crushed nuts or sugar-free chocolate chips if you want texture. It's basically a guilt-free sundae.

8. High-Protein Chocolate Mug Cake

Why It Rocks

Instant chocolate fix—microwave style. Using protein powder and minimal sugar keeps it from being a total macro landmine.

Ingredients (1 mug cake)

- 1 scoop chocolate protein powder
- 1 egg or 2 egg whites
- 2 tbsp unsweetened cocoa powder (optional if your protein is already chocolate)
- 2–4 tbsp milk (adjust thickness)
- Sweetener to taste

Method

1. **Mix** all ingredients in a microwave-safe mug.
2. **Microwave** ~45–60 seconds, watch so it doesn't overflow.
3. **Check** doneness; microwave in short bursts if still gooey.

Pro Tip

Top with a tiny spoonful of peanut butter or Greek yogurt for extra decadence. Don't overcook or it gets rubbery.

9. Protein Nachos

Why It Rocks
Nachos can be a cheat-meal minefield—but swap in baked tortilla chips, lean protein, and sensible cheese to get your fix without blowing your macros.

Ingredients (~2 servings)

- 6–8 oz lean ground turkey or chicken
- 1 tsp taco seasoning (DIY from Chapter 9)
- 2 cups baked tortilla chips
- ½ cup low-fat shredded cheese
- Toppings: diced tomatoes, jalapeños, salsa, Greek yogurt (instead of sour cream)

Method

1. **Brown** meat with taco seasoning.
2. **Arrange** chips on a baking sheet, top with meat and cheese.
3. **Broil** or bake briefly until cheese melts.
4. **Add** veggies, salsa, and yogurt.

Pro Tip
Skip drowning your nachos in cheese. A moderate sprinkle + bold seasonings can do wonders. Pile on veggies for volume without extra calories.

10. PB & Banana Quesadilla

Why It Rocks
Sweet, warm, protein-friendly snack or dessert. Whole-wheat tortilla, peanut butter, and bananas—simple, yet hits the spot.

Ingredients (Makes 1 quesadilla)

- 1 whole-wheat tortilla
- 1 tbsp peanut butter (natural)
- 1 small banana, sliced
- Optional: sprinkle of cinnamon

Method

1. **Spread** PB on half the tortilla, layer banana slices.
2. **Fold** tortilla in half.
3. **Cook** in a skillet on medium ~1–2 mins each side.

Pro Tip
Add a drizzle of honey or sugar-free chocolate sauce if you need extra sweetness. Tastes like a dessert, but with better macros than a donut run.

11. Protein Pancakes (Cheat Edition)

Why It Rocks
Fluffy pancakes can stay in your life if you up the protein and watch the syrup. Great for a **Sunday brunch** cheat that won't kill your weekly plan.

Ingredients (Makes ~4 pancakes)

- 1 scoop whey or casein protein (vanilla)
- ½ cup oats, blended into flour
- 1 egg (or 2 egg whites)
- ½ cup milk (low-fat or almond)
- 1 tsp baking powder

Method

1. **Combine** dry ingredients; mix in egg and milk.
2. **Stir** until batter is slightly thick.
3. **Cook** on a non-stick skillet ~1–2 mins per side.

Pro Tip
Top with fresh fruit, Greek yogurt, or sugar-free syrup if you must. Skip drowning them in butter to keep it cheat-ish, not cheat-apocalypse.

12. Lean Philly Cheesesteak Wrap

Why It Rocks
Sometimes you crave a cheesesteak. Using lean steak and a whole-wheat wrap cuts carbs/fat, plus controlling the cheese is crucial.

Ingredients (Makes 1 wrap)

- 4–5 oz lean steak, thinly sliced (sirloin, flank)
- ¼ cup onions, peppers (sautéed)
- 1 slice reduced-fat provolone or mozzarella
- 1 whole-wheat tortilla
- Salt, pepper

Method

1. **Cook** steak strips with salt, pepper. Sauté onions/peppers.
2. **Layer** on a tortilla, top with cheese.
3. **Broil** or microwave briefly to melt cheese. Roll it up.

Pro Tip

Go easy on the oil when sautéing. A quick spray of cooking oil and some seasoning is enough for a flavorful, less-greasy meal.

13. Healthy-ish Brownies

Why It Rocks

Rich chocolate brownies that won't explode your calorie count. Using applesauce or Greek yogurt, plus some protein powder, keeps it from becoming sugar overload.

Ingredients (~9 brownies)

- ½ cup whole-wheat flour
- ¼ cup cocoa powder (unsweetened)
- ¼ cup chocolate protein powder (optional)
- ½ cup applesauce (unsweetened) or Greek yogurt
- 1 egg
- ⅓ cup sweetener (sugar, stevia, etc.)
- ½ tsp baking powder
- Pinch of salt

Method

1. **Preheat** oven to 350°F (175°C). Grease an 8×8 pan.
2. **Mix** dry ingredients in a bowl. Add wet ingredients.
3. **Stir** until combined; pour into pan.
4. **Bake** ~15–18 minutes (don't overbake!).

Pro Tip

Cool completely before cutting. For extra chocolate kick, add sugar-free chocolate chips on top.

14. Cauliflower Crust Pizza

Why It Rocks
Pizza #2? Why not. Cauliflower crust cuts carbs while letting you load up on sauce, cheese, and toppings—still a cheat, but a lighter one.

Ingredients (Makes 1 medium pizza)

- 1 head cauliflower, riced (or buy pre-riced)
- ½ cup shredded mozzarella (low-fat)
- 1 egg
- ½ tsp oregano, ½ tsp garlic powder
- Toppings: sauce, cheese, veggies, lean meats

Method

1. **Preheat** oven to 400°F (200°C).
2. **Microwave** riced cauliflower ~4–5 mins; squeeze out moisture.
3. **Mix** cauliflower with egg, cheese, seasonings.
4. **Form** crust on a baking sheet; bake ~15 mins.
5. **Top** with sauce, cheese, etc. Bake ~5 more mins.

Pro Tip
Squeeze the cauliflower *really well* or the crust might get soggy. A dishtowel works wonders for removing excess water.

15. Grilled Fruit & Greek Yogurt Parfait

Why It Rocks
Dessert doesn't have to be cake. Grilled peaches, pineapple, or apples add a caramelized sweetness, paired with high-protein yogurt for a refreshing treat.

Ingredients (Makes 2 parfaits)

- 2 peaches (or pineapple rings, or apple slices)
- 2 cups plain Greek yogurt
- 1–2 tbsp honey or sweetener
- Cinnamon (optional)

Method

1. **Slice** fruit; grill or pan-sear until lightly caramelized.
2. **Layer** yogurt and fruit in cups.

3. **Drizzle** honey or sprinkle cinnamon if you want extra sweetness.

Pro Tip
Try grilling the fruit on high heat just a minute each side—enough to get those grill marks and intensify the natural sugars.

Bottom Line

Cheat meals don't have to trash your macros or bury your gains. With these **15** indulgent-but-smart ideas, you can satisfy cravings, stay in control, and bounce right back to your regular plan without a ton of guilt. So **cheat** responsibly—indulge, enjoy, and keep on crushing. Because a controlled cheat is just another step on the path, not a destructive detour. Now go feast wisely.

CHAPTER 11: NO STALLS, NO PLATEAUS— FIXING YOUR WEAK POINTS

Got trouble spots? Hit a plateau? Handle it. We'll cover adjustments and strategies for when the scale or the mirror stops playing nice.

Let's get real for a second: hitting a plateau **sucks**. You're killing it in the gym, staying loyal to your macros, and for a while, the results were coming in hot. But then—**bam!**—everything comes to a screeching halt. The scale refuses to budge, the mirror doesn't show you any love, and suddenly, you're questioning why you're even bothering. Sound familiar? Good. Because this chapter is here to slap you awake and remind you that **plateaus are a challenge, not a death sentence**.

What's Really Happening?

Plateaus aren't magic; they're science. Your body is a **master adapter**—and that's both a blessing and a curse. When you start a new routine, your muscles and metabolism are like, "Whoa, what's this? Better get stronger and leaner to keep up." But over time, your body adjusts. It gets efficient at what you're throwing at it, and suddenly, the workouts that used to wreck you feel like a walk in the park. The same goes for your diet—your metabolism catches on, and progress slows.

The good news? You're not stuck. You're just being called to **level up**, to push past the lazy efficiency your body has settled into and make it work harder again.

Spotting the Problem

Before you go into full panic mode, let's pinpoint where things are going sideways. Ask yourself these brutally honest questions:

- **Have you gotten too comfortable?** Are you still lifting the same weights or eating the same meals you started with?
- **Are you tracking everything?** That "little extra" peanut butter or uncounted weekend cocktail might be sneaking into your macros.
- **Are you resting enough—or too much?** Recovery is key, but so is consistency. Missed workouts or poor sleep = stalled progress.
- **Are you being patient?** Let's be real: not seeing changes after a week doesn't mean you've hit a plateau. Give it a couple of weeks before declaring a crisis.

Once you've spotted the weak link, you're halfway to crushing it.

146

The Mindset Shift: Stop Whining, Start Winning

Here's the deal: plateaus aren't proof that you've failed—they're proof that you've improved. If your routine wasn't working, you wouldn't have plateaued in the first place. The only way to break through is to **change the game**. That means tweaking your approach, pushing harder, and dialing in your focus. Plateaus separate the people who are **serious** from the ones who just like to dabble. Which one are you? Exactly.

What's Next?

In the next sections, we'll tackle exactly how to fix your weak points, ramp up your routine, and keep climbing when it feels like you've hit the ceiling. Whether it's adjusting your macros, switching up your training, or tightening your recovery game, we've got a blueprint to blast through the plateau and keep those gains rolling.

No more excuses, no more "I guess this is good enough." Let's crank it up and get back to smashing goals like the unstoppable badass you are. Flip the page—it's time to handle business.

Recipes Included: 10 specialized recipes (like higher-calorie bulking meals or lean-down tweaks)

Here are **10 specialized recipes** crafted to help you **break through plateaus**, whether you're trying to **bulk up** or **lean down**. Each recipe is packed with flavor, carefully designed to target your goals, and stupidly simple to prepare. These are your secret weapons when the scale or mirror isn't showing love. **No excuses, no compromises—just results.**

1. Beast Mode Breakfast Bowl (Higher-Calorie Bulking)

Why It Rocks
Perfect for kicking off a day of **serious eating** when you're chasing gains. This bowl is loaded with protein, healthy fats, and carbs to fuel your lifts.

Ingredients (Serves 1)

- 1 cup cooked oats
- 1 scoop vanilla protein powder
- 1 tbsp almond butter
- ½ banana, sliced
- 1 tbsp honey
- 1 tbsp chopped nuts (walnuts or almonds)

Method

1. **Cook** oats as directed. Stir in protein powder while it's still hot.
2. **Top** with banana slices, almond butter, honey, and chopped nuts.

Pro Tip

Double the batch, store in the fridge, and reheat for fast bulk-friendly breakfasts during the week.

2. Shredded Chicken Power Bowl (Lean-Down Tweaks)

Why It Rocks

Lean protein, low carbs, and a load of veggies to keep you full without weighing you down. Perfect for cutting while staying energized.

Ingredients (Serves 1)

- 4 oz shredded chicken breast
- 1 cup mixed greens (spinach, arugula, kale)
- ½ cup steamed broccoli
- ¼ avocado, sliced
- 1 tbsp olive oil + lemon juice for dressing

Method

1. **Assemble** greens, broccoli, chicken, and avocado in a bowl.
2. **Drizzle** olive oil and lemon juice on top. Toss lightly.

Pro Tip

Prep shredded chicken in bulk on Sundays—add different seasonings (chipotle, garlic-herb) to keep meals interesting all week.

3. Monster Mass Gainer Smoothie (Higher-Calorie Bulking)

Why It Rocks

Packed with **clean calories** to hit your macros fast. This is liquid muscle fuel—ideal for anyone who "can't eat enough" during a bulk.

Ingredients (Serves 1)

- 1 cup whole milk (or almond milk for lighter calories)
- 1 scoop chocolate protein powder
- 2 tbsp peanut butter
- ½ banana
- 1 tbsp honey
- 1 tsp cocoa powder (optional for extra chocolate flavor)

Method

1. **Blend** everything until smooth. Adjust thickness with more milk or ice.

Pro Tip
Add ¼ cup oats or a handful of spinach for extra carbs or micronutrients without changing the taste much.

4. Spicy Sriracha Salmon Bowl (Lean-Down Tweaks)

Why It Rocks
Low-calorie but high-flavor. This bowl gives you healthy fats, protein, and just enough spice to make eating clean exciting.

Ingredients (Serves 1)

- 4 oz baked salmon
- 1 cup cauliflower rice
- 1 cup steamed asparagus
- 1 tbsp sriracha mixed with 1 tsp soy sauce

Method

1. **Cook** salmon and cauliflower rice as desired.
2. **Assemble** salmon, rice, and asparagus in a bowl.
3. **Drizzle** sriracha-soy sauce mix over everything.

Pro Tip
Roast the asparagus with a pinch of garlic powder for added flavor.

5. Protein-Packed Egg & Veggie Scramble (Either Goal)

Why It Rocks
A versatile, quick meal. Adjust the carb add-ons (toast, potatoes) depending on whether you're bulking or cutting.

Ingredients (Serves 1)

- 3 egg whites + 1 whole egg
- ½ cup diced bell peppers
- ½ cup spinach
- 1 tsp olive oil
- Optional for bulking: 1 slice whole-grain toast

Method

1. **Sauté** veggies in olive oil until softened.
2. **Add** eggs, scramble until cooked through.
3. **Serve** with or without toast depending on your goal.

Pro Tip
Sprinkle with hot sauce or a touch of shredded low-fat cheese for extra kick.

6. Big Batch Beef & Sweet Potato Hash (Higher-Calorie Bulking)

Why It Rocks
Great for meal prep. Sweet potatoes provide slow-digesting carbs, while lean ground beef brings the protein.

Ingredients (Serves ~4)

- 1 lb lean ground beef
- 2 medium sweet potatoes, diced
- 1 cup diced onions and bell peppers
- 1 tbsp olive oil
- Salt, pepper, paprika

Method

1. **Cook** sweet potatoes in olive oil over medium heat until tender. Remove from pan.
2. **Brown** beef with onions and peppers. Season with paprika, salt, pepper.
3. **Combine** potatoes with beef mixture.

Pro Tip

Store in containers for up to 4 days. Add a fried egg on top for bonus protein.

7. Turkey Meatballs with Zoodles (Lean-Down Tweaks)

Why It Rocks

Meatballs without the carb-heavy pasta. Zoodles (zucchini noodles) keep the dish light while still feeling hearty.

Ingredients (Serves 2)

- 8 turkey meatballs (see Chapter 8 for recipe)
- 2 medium zucchini, spiralized
- ½ cup marinara sauce (low-sugar)
- 1 tsp olive oil

Method

1. **Heat** meatballs and marinara in a pan.
2. **Sauté** zoodles lightly in olive oil (~2 mins).
3. **Combine** zoodles with sauce and meatballs.

Pro Tip

Sprinkle with a pinch of Parmesan or red pepper flakes for added flavor.

8. Steak & Quinoa Power Plate (Higher-Calorie Bulking)

Why It Rocks

Lean steak + quinoa = a hearty meal with high protein, clean carbs, and a touch of healthy fats.

Ingredients (Serves 1)

- 6 oz lean steak (sirloin, flank)
- ½ cup cooked quinoa
- 1 cup roasted broccoli
- 1 tsp olive oil

Method

1. **Cook** steak to preferred doneness; let it rest and slice thinly.
2. **Roast** broccoli with olive oil, salt, and pepper.

3. **Plate** steak, quinoa, and broccoli.

Pro Tip
Quinoa can be cooked in bulk for the week. Add a drizzle of lemon juice or soy sauce for extra flavor.

9. Creamy Protein Smoothie Bowl (Lean-Down Tweaks)

Why It Rocks
A dessert-like treat that fits your macros. High in protein and low in carbs/fat when you keep the toppings light.

Ingredients (Serves 1)

- 1 scoop vanilla protein powder
- 1 cup unsweetened almond milk
- ½ cup frozen berries
- Optional toppings: 1 tsp chia seeds, a few almond slivers

Method

1. **Blend** protein powder, milk, and berries until smooth and thick.
2. **Pour** into a bowl; top with light toppings.

Pro Tip
Freeze the berries solid for a thicker, ice-cream-like consistency.

10. Chicken Stir-Fry with Peanut Sauce (Higher-Calorie Bulking)

Why It Rocks
Quick, versatile, and packed with protein, healthy fats, and carbs to keep you fueled during a bulk.

Ingredients (Serves 2)

- 8 oz chicken breast, diced
- 2 cups mixed veggies (bell peppers, broccoli, snap peas)
- 1 tbsp olive oil
- 2 tbsp peanut butter
- 1 tbsp soy sauce

- 1 tsp sriracha (optional for spice)

Method

1. **Cook** chicken in olive oil; remove once browned.
2. **Stir-fry** veggies in the same pan.
3. **Mix** peanut butter, soy sauce, sriracha with a splash of water for sauce.
4. **Combine** chicken, veggies, and sauce in the pan.

Pro Tip
Serve over rice if bulking or cauliflower rice if cutting. Adjust the peanut butter amount to fit your calorie needs.

Final Thoughts

These **10 recipes** are your arsenal for crushing plateaus and targeting your specific goals—whether you're bulking up with calorie-packed meals or leaning down with clean, satisfying plates. **Plan, prep, and execute**, and let your food work as hard as you do. Because here, every bite matters.

CHAPTER 12: FINAL PUSH—STAY HUNGRY, STAY RECKLESS

Wrap it up with motivational smack talk to keep you laser-focused. Remember, muscle isn't built in a day—and this chapter makes sure you don't quit on day two.

Let's cut the fluff: **this is where most people quit.** They've made some progress, gotten comfortable, and suddenly, the fire fizzles out. The grind feels endless, the excitement fades, and all those goals start looking like distant mirages instead of the concrete reality they're supposed to be. Sound familiar? That's because the final stretch is where the real battle happens—not in the first week when you're hyped, but in the grind of week 8, 12, or 52 when every rep, every meal, every decision feels like a choice between staying on track or throwing in the towel.

But here's the truth: **this isn't the end of the journey.** This is the beginning of a lifestyle. If you want long-term success—if you want to keep smashing PRs, building strength, and sculpting the body you've always wanted—then you've got to stay hungry. Hungry for progress, for growth, for a better version of yourself. And you've got to stay reckless—not reckless as in careless, but reckless in your refusal to settle, your willingness to push harder when others back down, and your obsession with showing up no matter how tough it gets.

Where Most People Screw It Up

By now, you've got the tools. You've got recipes to fuel your goals, strategies to crush plateaus, and workouts that deliver results. So why do people still fail? Because they lose focus. They let boredom creep in, fall back into old habits, or start coasting because they think they've "made it." But let me tell you something: **there's no finish line** when it comes to being your best self. You don't just hit a goal and stop—you find a new one, then another, and another after that. **You're never done.**

The Power of Small Wins

Here's the kicker: staying hungry doesn't mean chasing massive milestones every day. It's about stacking **small wins**—one after another—until they add up to something unstoppable. Whether it's an extra rep at the gym, a new recipe you nailed, or resisting the junk food that used to own you, every choice matters. Every single one. Celebrate those wins, because they're the bricks that build your foundation.

When the Motivation Fades

Let's be honest—motivation is overrated. It's easy to feel fired up when everything's new, but when the routine sets in, you need more than a pump-up playlist to keep going. You need **discipline**. That means showing up even when you don't feel like it. Cooking the meals, tracking the macros, hitting the gym—even on the days when Netflix and takeout are calling your name. Because guess what? The people who succeed aren't the ones who are always motivated—they're the ones who refuse to quit.

What's Next?

This chapter is your **wake-up call**. It's here to remind you that this isn't the end—it's the next level. We'll talk about how to set new goals, adjust your approach as your body evolves, and keep pushing when the honeymoon phase is long gone. Because you didn't come this far just to stop now, right? Let's lock in, level up, and finish strong.

Flip the page and let's finish what we started—hungry, reckless, and ready for whatever comes next.

Recipes Included: A curated "best of" list (about 10–15 crowd favorites) to motivate you through the home stretch

Below is your **"best of" list**—a handpicked selection of **10 crowd-favorite recipes** that have carried readers (and their gains) through the toughest stretches. These aren't just meals; they're the ones you keep coming back to when you need something **easy, satisfying, and downright delicious**. They're here to remind you why you started and to keep you crushing it until the very end.

1. Buffalo Chicken Protein Wraps

Why It Rocks
Spicy, savory, and ridiculously easy to throw together. These wraps hit your protein goals without wrecking your calorie count.

Ingredients (Serves 1)

- 4 oz cooked chicken breast, shredded
- 1 tbsp hot sauce (Frank's or your fave)
- 1 tbsp plain Greek yogurt
- 1 whole-wheat tortilla
- Optional: shredded lettuce, diced celery

Method

1. **Mix** chicken, hot sauce, and yogurt.
2. **Assemble** in the tortilla with lettuce and celery.
3. **Wrap** and devour.

Pro Tip
Switch out the tortilla for lettuce wraps if you're cutting carbs. Same flavor, fewer calories.

2. High-Protein Pizza Bagels

Why It Rocks
Quick, customizable, and feels like a cheat meal without being one. Perfect for a busy weeknight or post-workout fuel.

Ingredients (Serves 1)

- 2 whole-grain bagel halves
- 2 tbsp low-sugar marinara sauce
- ¼ cup low-fat mozzarella cheese
- 2–3 slices turkey pepperoni
- Optional: diced bell peppers, mushrooms

Method

1. **Preheat** oven to 400°F (200°C).
2. **Spread** marinara on each bagel half. Top with cheese, pepperoni, and optional veggies.
3. **Bake** ~8–10 minutes until cheese is melted.

Pro Tip
Double the batch for meal prep. They reheat like a dream in the oven or air fryer.

3. Overnight Protein Oats

Why It Rocks
Minimal effort, maximum gains. A creamy, sweet breakfast that's ready to grab and go.

Ingredients (Serves 1)

- ½ cup rolled oats
- 1 scoop vanilla protein powder

- ½ cup unsweetened almond milk
- 1 tbsp chia seeds
- Optional: sliced banana, berries, or a drizzle of almond butter

Method

1. **Combine** all ingredients in a jar or container.
2. **Chill** overnight in the fridge.
3. **Top** with fruit or nut butter in the morning.

Pro Tip
For variety, swap protein flavors or stir in cocoa powder for a chocolate twist.

4. Sweet Potato Protein Pancakes

Why It Rocks
Fluffy, slightly sweet pancakes with a nutrient-dense punch. Great for a weekend breakfast or post-workout treat.

Ingredients (Serves 2)

- 1 cup mashed sweet potato
- 1 scoop vanilla or unflavored protein powder
- 2 egg whites
- 1 tsp cinnamon
- 1 tsp baking powder

Method

1. **Mix** all ingredients into a smooth batter.
2. **Cook** in a nonstick pan over medium heat, ~2 mins per side.

Pro Tip
Top with sugar-free syrup or a dollop of Greek yogurt for extra flavor.

5. One-Pan Lemon Garlic Salmon

Why It Rocks
Packed with omega-3s and bursting with flavor, this salmon dish feels fancy but is stupidly easy to make.

Ingredients (Serves 2)

- 2 salmon fillets (~4 oz each)
- 1 tbsp olive oil
- 2 cloves garlic, minced
- Juice of 1 lemon
- 1 cup asparagus spears

Method

1. **Preheat** oven to 375°F (190°C).
2. **Arrange** salmon and asparagus on a sheet pan. Drizzle with olive oil, garlic, and lemon juice.
3. **Bake** ~12–15 minutes until salmon flakes easily.

Pro Tip
Add a sprinkle of red pepper flakes if you like a bit of heat.

6. Chili-Lime Chicken Bowls

Why It Rocks
Zesty and satisfying, these bowls are perfect for meal prep or a quick lunch.

Ingredients (Serves 2)

- 8 oz chicken breast, grilled or baked
- 1 cup cooked brown rice
- 1 cup steamed broccoli
- Juice of 1 lime
- 1 tsp chili powder

Method

1. **Slice** chicken and toss with lime juice and chili powder.
2. **Assemble** bowls with rice, broccoli, and chicken.

Pro Tip
Top with a dollop of plain Greek yogurt for a creamy finish.

7. Protein-Packed Veggie Stir-Fry

Why It Rocks
A quick, colorful dish that's high in protein and packed with flavor.

Ingredients (Serves 2)

- 1 block firm tofu, cubed (or 8 oz chicken/shrimp)
- 2 cups mixed veggies (broccoli, bell peppers, snap peas)
- 2 tbsp low-sodium soy sauce
- 1 tsp sesame oil

Method

1. **Sear** tofu or protein in sesame oil.
2. **Stir-fry** veggies until tender-crisp. Add soy sauce.
3. **Combine** and serve hot.

Pro Tip
Serve over cauliflower rice if cutting or jasmine rice if bulking.

8. Turkey Taco Lettuce Wraps

Why It Rocks
All the taco flavor, none of the carb bomb. Great for quick lunches or party snacks.

Ingredients (Serves 2)

- 8 oz lean ground turkey
- 1 tsp taco seasoning
- 1 cup chopped lettuce leaves (as wraps)
- Optional: diced tomatoes, shredded cheese, salsa

Method

1. **Cook** turkey with taco seasoning.
2. **Scoop** into lettuce leaves and top with optional ingredients.

Pro Tip
Swap lettuce for low-carb tortillas if you want a bit more structure.

9. Creamy Avocado Protein Smoothie

Why It Rocks
Smooth, rich, and packed with healthy fats and protein. Perfect for a quick, filling snack.

Ingredients (Serves 1)

- ½ avocado
- 1 scoop vanilla or chocolate protein powder
- 1 cup unsweetened almond milk
- 1 tsp honey (optional)

Method

1. **Blend** everything until smooth. Adjust thickness with milk or ice.

Pro Tip
Add a handful of spinach for extra greens—you won't taste it, but your body will thank you.

10. High-Protein Peanut Butter Cups

Why It Rocks
Dessert that feels indulgent but delivers on protein. Perfect for curbing late-night cravings.

Ingredients (Makes 6 cups)

- ½ cup natural peanut butter
- 1 scoop chocolate protein powder
- ¼ cup melted dark chocolate

Method

1. **Mix** peanut butter and protein powder into a smooth paste.
2. **Layer** melted chocolate and PB mix in silicone molds or muffin liners.
3. **Chill** in fridge until set.

Pro Tip
Use sugar-free chocolate for fewer calories without losing the indulgent vibe.

Final Word

These **recipes** are here to remind you that sticking to your goals doesn't have to suck. They're flavorful, easy, and proven favorites for crushing plateaus, satisfying cravings, and keeping your macros on point. Use them to finish strong, fuel your workouts, and celebrate how far you've come—without ever losing sight of where you're going. **Stay hungry. Stay reckless. Keep crushing it.**

The No-Excuses Bonus: 30 Days to Wreck Plateaus and Build a Savage New You

Structured in 5-Day Segments for Maximum Focus and Flexibility

Welcome to your **5-Day Body Reset Challenge**, where excuses are off the table, and action takes center stage. This isn't a fluffy detox or some overpriced juice cleanse. This is a **hard-hitting, no-BS plan** designed to help you regain control, smash through plateaus, and light a fire under your progress. It's short, focused, and effective—exactly what you need to reignite your drive.

Each day, you'll have:

- A **killer workout** (no gym required—your body is the machine).
- A **focused meal plan** built from the recipes in this book.
- A **challenge task** to sharpen your discipline and mindset.

You're here to win, not coast. Let's get to it.

Day 1: The Wake-Up Call

Workout

- **Warm-Up:** 5 minutes of dynamic stretches (arm circles, lunges, high knees).
- **Circuit (3 rounds):**
    - Push-Ups (as many as you can in 30 seconds)
    - Bodyweight Squats (15 reps)
    - Plank Hold (30 seconds)
    - Jumping Jacks (30 seconds)
- **Cool-Down:** Stretch for 5 minutes.

Meal Plan

- **Breakfast:** Overnight Protein Oats (Chapter 4)
- **Lunch:** Shredded Chicken Power Bowl (Chapter 3)
- **Dinner:** Spicy Sriracha Salmon Bowl (Chapter 6)
- **Snack:** Greek Yogurt with a drizzle of honey and a handful of berries.

Challenge Task

Write down **three specific goals** you want to achieve in the next 30 days. Be clear—"lose weight" isn't enough. Try "drop 2% body fat" or "add 20 lbs to my bench press." Post it somewhere you'll see daily.

Day 2: Dominate the Day

Workout

- **Warm-Up:** 5 minutes of light jogging or jump rope.
- **Circuit (3 rounds):**
  - Burpees (10 reps)
  - Lunges (10 reps per leg)
  - Mountain Climbers (30 seconds)
  - Bicycle Crunches (30 seconds)
- **Cool-Down:** Stretch for 5 minutes.

Meal Plan

- **Breakfast:** Sweet Potato Protein Pancakes (Chapter 4)
- **Lunch:** Chili-Lime Chicken Bowl (Chapter 6)
- **Dinner:** One-Pan Lemon Garlic Salmon (Chapter 6)
- **Snack:** High-Protein Peanut Butter Cups (Chapter 10)

Challenge Task

Identify **one bad habit** that's holding you back (skipping workouts, mindless snacking, staying up late). Write it down and commit to eliminating it for the rest of the challenge. No exceptions.

Day 3: Push Through the Burn

Workout

- **Warm-Up:** 5 minutes of light cardio.
- **Circuit (4 rounds):**
  - Push-Ups to Failure
  - Jump Squats (15 reps)
  - Plank with Shoulder Taps (30 seconds)
  - High Knees (30 seconds)
- **Cool-Down:** Foam rolling or stretching for 5 minutes.

Meal Plan

- **Breakfast:** Beast Mode Breakfast Bowl (Chapter 3)
- **Lunch:** Turkey Taco Lettuce Wraps (Chapter 7)
- **Dinner:** Steak & Quinoa Power Plate (Chapter 6)
- **Snack:** Protein-Packed Egg & Veggie Scramble (Chapter 5)

Challenge Task

Add **10 minutes of mindfulness** before bed. No phones, no screens—just sit, breathe, and reflect on your day. The goal is to build focus and clarity.

Day 4: Break the Plateau

Workout

- **Warm-Up:** 5 minutes of mobility drills (hip circles, arm swings, etc.).
- **Strength & Core (3 rounds):**
  - Bodyweight Deadlifts (15 reps)
  - Side Plank Hold (30 seconds per side)
  - Tricep Dips (15 reps)
  - Flutter Kicks (30 seconds)
- **Cool-Down:** Stretch and deep breathing for 5 minutes.

Meal Plan

- **Breakfast:** High-Protein Pancakes (Chapter 4)
- **Lunch:** Protein-Packed Veggie Stir-Fry (Chapter 7)
- **Dinner:** Big Batch Beef & Sweet Potato Hash (Chapter 6)
- **Snack:** Protein Cheesecake Cups (Chapter 10)

Challenge Task

Plan your meals for the next week. Use recipes from the book and write out your grocery list. Planning ahead eliminates excuses and sets you up for success.

Day 5: Finish Strong

Workout

- **Warm-Up:** 5 minutes of dynamic stretches.
- **Final Challenge (4 rounds):**
  - Burpees (12 reps)
  - Push-Ups (to failure)
  - Bodyweight Squats (20 reps)
  - Plank Hold (45 seconds)
- **Cool-Down:** Stretch and reflect on how far you've come.

Meal Plan

- **Breakfast:** Protein Mug Cake (Chapter 7)

- **Lunch:** Shredded Chicken Salad with Avocado (Chapter 3)
- **Dinner:** Cauliflower Crust Pizza (Chapter 10)
- **Snack:** Creamy Avocado Protein Smoothie (Chapter 7)

Challenge Task

Reflect on the past five days. Write down:

1. **What you've learned** about your habits, strengths, and areas to improve.
2. **One thing you're proud of** achieving during the challenge.
3. **Your next goal**—because this doesn't stop here.

Final Push

You've crushed this 5-day reset, but this is just the beginning. Keep stacking those wins, pushing your limits, and building the body and mindset you deserve. **Stay hungry, stay reckless, and keep dominating.** Let's go!

5-Day Body Reset Challenge: Days 6–10

Day 6: Build Momentum

Workout

- **Warm-Up:** 5 minutes of dynamic stretches (focus on hips, shoulders, and core).
- **Circuit (3 rounds):**
    - Jump Squats (15 reps)
    - Push-Ups with a Clap (or regular push-ups if needed) – 10 reps
    - Plank with Hip Dips (30 seconds)
    - Mountain Climbers (30 seconds)
- **Cool-Down:** Stretch for 5 minutes, focusing on hamstrings and shoulders.

Meal Plan

- **Breakfast:** Overnight Protein Oats with Peanut Butter (Chapter 4)
- **Lunch:** High-Protein Pizza Bagels (Chapter 10)
- **Dinner:** Spicy Sriracha Salmon Bowl (Chapter 6)
- **Snack:** Roasted Chickpeas with Smoky Paprika (Chapter 9)

Challenge Task

Make a list of **three things that motivate you**—whether it's family, fitness goals, or smashing your personal best at the gym. Keep this list where you can see it every day as a reminder to stay focused.

Day 7: Crush the Week

Workout

- **Warm-Up:** 5 minutes of jogging or jump rope.
- **Circuit (4 rounds):**
    - Bodyweight Deadlifts (15 reps)
    - Side Plank Hold (30 seconds per side)
    - Jump Lunges (10 reps per leg)
    - Bicycle Crunches (30 seconds)
- **Cool-Down:** Foam rolling or gentle yoga stretches for 5 minutes.

Meal Plan

- **Breakfast:** Protein Pancakes with Berry Topping (Chapter 4)
- **Lunch:** Chili-Lime Chicken Bowl (Chapter 6)
- **Dinner:** One-Pan Lemon Garlic Salmon with Steamed Veggies (Chapter 6)
- **Snack:** Greek Yogurt with Dark Chocolate Chips (Chapter 7)

Challenge Task

Set a **mini goal** for the next three days. Whether it's drinking more water, hitting every workout, or resisting late-night snacks, commit to one small win and execute like a pro.

Day 8: Fuel and Focus

Workout

- **Warm-Up:** 5 minutes of light dynamic stretches.
- **Circuit (3 rounds):**
    - Burpees (12 reps)
    - Plank-to-Push-Up Transitions (10 reps)
    - High Knees (30 seconds)
    - Tricep Dips (15 reps)
- **Cool-Down:** Stretch and deep breathing for 5 minutes.

Meal Plan

- **Breakfast:** Sweet Potato Protein Pancakes (Chapter 4)
- **Lunch:** Turkey Taco Lettuce Wraps with Salsa (Chapter 7)
- **Dinner:** Big Batch Beef & Sweet Potato Hash (Chapter 6)
- **Snack:** High-Protein Chocolate Mug Cake (Chapter 7)

Challenge Task

Declutter your kitchen. Get rid of processed junk, snacks you know derail you, and anything that doesn't align with your goals. Stock your fridge with clean, whole foods that keep you on track.

Day 9: Dig Deeper

Workout

- **Warm-Up:** 5 minutes of mobility drills (hip circles, arm swings, etc.).
- **Circuit (3 rounds):**
  - Jump Squats (15 reps)
  - Plank Holds with Shoulder Taps (30 seconds)
  - Push-Ups to Failure
  - Flutter Kicks (30 seconds)
- **Cool-Down:** Gentle stretching, focusing on quads and shoulders.

Meal Plan

- **Breakfast:** Beast Mode Breakfast Bowl (Chapter 3)
- **Lunch:** Shredded Chicken Salad with Avocado Dressing (Chapter 7)
- **Dinner:** Protein-Packed Veggie Stir-Fry (Chapter 6)
- **Snack:** Protein Cheesecake Cups (Chapter 10)

Challenge Task

Reflect on your progress so far. Write down:

1. **What's working**—the habits and meals that make sticking to this challenge easier.
2. **What's not working**—adjustments you need to make.

Day 10: Finish Like a Beast

Workout

- **Warm-Up:** 5 minutes of dynamic cardio (jogging, high knees, etc.).
- **Final Challenge (4 rounds):**
  - Burpees (15 reps)
  - Push-Ups with Hold at the Bottom (10 reps)
  - Bodyweight Squats (20 reps)
  - Plank Hold (1 minute)
- **Cool-Down:** Full-body stretch, focusing on hamstrings, hips, and shoulders.

Meal Plan

- **Breakfast:** Overnight Protein Oats with Fresh Berries (Chapter 4)

- **Lunch:** Protein Nachos with Turkey (Chapter 10)
- **Dinner:** Cauliflower Crust Pizza with Lean Toppings (Chapter 10)
- **Snack:** Creamy Avocado Protein Smoothie (Chapter 7)

Challenge Task

Plan your next **30-day goal**. Whether it's a new PR at the gym, leaning out further, or maintaining your progress, **write it down**. Break it into weekly action steps and commit to continuing the work.

Final Words

You've powered through **10 days of discipline, focus, and effort**. This reset wasn't just about the food or the workouts—it was about proving to yourself that you can do hard things and come out stronger. Now, take what you've built and keep going. Remember: **stay hungry, stay reckless, and keep crushing it.** Let's go.

5-Day Body Reset Challenge: Days 11–15

Day 11: Reignite the Fire

Workout

- **Warm-Up:** 5 minutes of dynamic stretches (focus on full-body movements).
- **Circuit (3 rounds):**
    - Jump Lunges (10 reps per leg)
    - Plank-to-Push-Up Transitions (10 reps)
    - Burpees (10 reps)
    - Flutter Kicks (30 seconds)
- **Cool-Down:** Stretch and foam roll, focusing on hamstrings and shoulders.

Meal Plan

- **Breakfast:** Protein Pancakes with Peanut Butter Drizzle (Chapter 4)
- **Lunch:** Chili-Lime Chicken Bowl (Chapter 6)
- **Dinner:** Spicy Sriracha Salmon Bowl with Roasted Veggies (Chapter 6)
- **Snack:** Greek Yogurt Ranch Dip with Veggie Sticks (Chapter 7)

Challenge Task

Write down **3 new habits** you've developed during this challenge. Reflect on how they've helped you so far and commit to keeping them part of your routine moving forward.

Day 12: Double Down on Discipline

Workout

- **Warm-Up:** 5 minutes of light cardio (jogging or jump rope).
- **Circuit (4 rounds):**
  - Bodyweight Deadlifts (15 reps)
  - Tricep Dips (15 reps)
  - Jump Squats (12 reps)
  - Side Plank Holds (30 seconds per side)
- **Cool-Down:** Stretch for 5 minutes, focusing on quads and lower back.

Meal Plan

- **Breakfast:** Overnight Protein Oats with Dark Chocolate Chips (Chapter 4)
- **Lunch:** Protein-Packed Veggie Stir-Fry (Chapter 7)
- **Dinner:** One-Pan Lemon Garlic Salmon with Steamed Broccoli (Chapter 6)
- **Snack:** High-Protein Peanut Butter Cups (Chapter 10)

Challenge Task

Identify one area where you're still **holding back**. Is it skipping reps, skimping on meal prep, or losing focus during workouts? Pinpoint it and **make a plan** to eliminate that weak spot starting today.

Day 13: Power Through the Plateau

Workout

- **Warm-Up:** 5 minutes of mobility drills (hip circles, arm swings, etc.).
- **Strength Circuit (3 rounds):**
  - Push-Ups to Failure
  - Bodyweight Squats (20 reps)
  - Plank with Shoulder Taps (30 seconds)
  - High Knees (30 seconds)
- **Cool-Down:** Foam roll or yoga stretches for 5 minutes.

Meal Plan

- **Breakfast:** Sweet Potato Protein Pancakes with Cinnamon (Chapter 4)
- **Lunch:** Shredded Chicken Power Bowl with Avocado (Chapter 3)
- **Dinner:** Big Batch Beef & Sweet Potato Hash (Chapter 6)
- **Snack:** Protein Mug Cake with a Drizzle of Honey (Chapter 7)

Challenge Task

Take 15 minutes to organize your **workout and meal schedule** for the next week. Write it down and commit to sticking with it—structure is your best ally.

Day 14: Build Confidence

Workout

- **Warm-Up:** 5 minutes of jogging or dynamic stretches.
- **Circuit (3 rounds):**
    - Burpees (12 reps)
    - Jump Lunges (10 reps per leg)
    - Plank Hold (45 seconds)
    - Flutter Kicks (30 seconds)
- **Cool-Down:** Stretch and deep breathing for 5 minutes.

Meal Plan

- **Breakfast:** Beast Mode Breakfast Bowl (Chapter 3)
- **Lunch:** Turkey Taco Lettuce Wraps (Chapter 7)
- **Dinner:** Protein-Packed Veggie Stir-Fry with Brown Rice (Chapter 6)
- **Snack:** Creamy Avocado Protein Smoothie (Chapter 7)

Challenge Task

Write down one **unexpected win** from this challenge so far—something you didn't plan for but achieved anyway. Use it as fuel to keep pushing forward.

Day 15: Finish Like a Legend

Workout

- **Warm-Up:** 5 minutes of light cardio.
- **Final Challenge (4 rounds):**
    - Burpees (15 reps)
    - Push-Ups with Hold at the Bottom (10 reps)
    - Bodyweight Deadlifts (20 reps)
    - Plank with Hip Dips (1 minute)
- **Cool-Down:** Full-body stretch, focusing on quads, hamstrings, and shoulders.

Meal Plan

- **Breakfast:** Overnight Protein Oats with Fresh Berries (Chapter 4)

- **Lunch:** Protein Nachos with Lean Turkey (Chapter 10)
- **Dinner:** Cauliflower Crust Pizza with Veggie Toppings (Chapter 10)
- **Snack:** High-Protein Cheesecake Cups with a Drizzle of Dark Chocolate (Chapter 10)

Challenge Task

Reflect on how far you've come in these 15 days. Write down:

1. **What you've achieved**—be specific.
2. **What you've learned** about your body, discipline, and mindset.
3. **Your next steps** to continue building momentum.

Final Words

15 days down, and you're stronger, sharper, and more focused than when you started. This wasn't just about workouts or recipes—it was about proving to yourself that you can rise to any challenge and come out on top. **Stay hungry, stay reckless, and never stop pushing for more.** Let's keep this energy going—you've got this.

5-Day Body Reset Challenge: Days 16–20

Day 16: Reinforce the Foundation

Workout

- **Warm-Up:** 5 minutes of light cardio (jogging, high knees).
- **Circuit (3 rounds):**
    - Jump Squats (15 reps)
    - Plank with Shoulder Taps (30 seconds)
    - Push-Ups (to failure)
    - Bicycle Crunches (30 seconds)
- **Cool-Down:** Stretch for 5 minutes, focusing on hips and hamstrings.

Meal Plan

- **Breakfast:** Sweet Potato Protein Pancakes (Chapter 4)
- **Lunch:** Chili-Lime Chicken Bowl (Chapter 6)
- **Dinner:** Spicy Sriracha Salmon with Steamed Veggies (Chapter 6)
- **Snack:** Protein-Packed Veggie Chips (Chapter 7)

Challenge Task

Review your progress from the last two weeks and write down **one thing you've improved on** that you didn't expect. Celebrate it by committing to pushing it further this week.

Day 17: Raise the Intensity

Workout

- **Warm-Up:** 5 minutes of mobility drills (hip circles, arm swings).
- **Circuit (4 rounds):**
  - Burpees (12 reps)
  - Jump Lunges (10 reps per leg)
  - Plank Holds (45 seconds)
  - Tricep Dips (15 reps)
- **Cool-Down:** Stretch and foam roll, focusing on shoulders and quads.

Meal Plan

- **Breakfast:** Protein Pancakes with Cinnamon and Honey (Chapter 4)
- **Lunch:** Turkey Taco Lettuce Wraps (Chapter 7)
- **Dinner:** Big Batch Beef & Sweet Potato Hash (Chapter 6)
- **Snack:** Greek Yogurt with Fresh Berries (Chapter 7)

Challenge Task

Set a **new short-term goal** for this week. Maybe it's hitting a specific number of reps, improving your form, or sticking to your meal plan 100%. Commit to it and track your progress daily.

Day 18: Keep the Momentum

Workout

- **Warm-Up:** 5 minutes of light cardio (jump rope or jogging).
- **Circuit (3 rounds):**
  - Push-Ups to Failure
  - Bodyweight Deadlifts (15 reps)
  - Flutter Kicks (30 seconds)
  - High Knees (30 seconds)
- **Cool-Down:** Foam rolling and light stretches for 5 minutes.

Meal Plan

- **Breakfast:** Overnight Protein Oats with Peanut Butter (Chapter 4)
- **Lunch:** Shredded Chicken Salad with Avocado (Chapter 3)
- **Dinner:** One-Pan Lemon Garlic Salmon with Roasted Broccoli (Chapter 6)
- **Snack:** High-Protein Chocolate Mug Cake (Chapter 10)

Challenge Task

Take 15 minutes to prepare for the next five days: write down your workouts, plan your meals, and ensure your fridge is stocked. **Preparation eliminates excuses.**

Day 19: Smash the Stagnation

Workout

- **Warm-Up:** 5 minutes of dynamic stretches.
- **Circuit (3 rounds):**
    - Burpees (15 reps)
    - Push-Ups with Hold at the Bottom (10 reps)
    - Jump Squats (12 reps)
    - Side Plank Holds (30 seconds per side)
- **Cool-Down:** Stretch and deep breathing for 5 minutes.

Meal Plan

- **Breakfast:** Beast Mode Breakfast Bowl (Chapter 3)
- **Lunch:** Chili-Lime Chicken Bowl with Brown Rice (Chapter 6)
- **Dinner:** Protein-Packed Veggie Stir-Fry (Chapter 7)
- **Snack:** Peanut Butter Protein Bars (Chapter 7)

Challenge Task

Reflect on how your mindset has shifted during this challenge. Write down **three ways you've grown mentally**—whether it's stronger discipline, better focus, or newfound motivation.

Day 20: Cross the Finish Line

Workout

- **Warm-Up:** 5 minutes of light jogging or mobility drills.
- **Final Challenge (4 rounds):**
    - Burpees (15 reps)
    - Push-Ups to Failure
    - Bodyweight Deadlifts (20 reps)
    - Plank with Hip Dips (1 minute)
- **Cool-Down:** Full-body stretch, focusing on quads, hamstrings, and shoulders.

Meal Plan

- **Breakfast:** Protein Pancakes with Fresh Berries (Chapter 4)

- **Lunch:** Protein Nachos with Lean Turkey (Chapter 10)
- **Dinner:** Cauliflower Crust Pizza with Veggie Toppings (Chapter 10)
- **Snack:** Creamy Avocado Protein Smoothie (Chapter 7)

Challenge Task

Take a moment to reflect on your **20-day journey**. Write down:

1. **Your biggest accomplishments.**
2. **What you've learned about yourself.**
3. **How you'll carry this momentum forward into the next phase.**

Final Words

You've made it to **Day 20**, and you're not just stronger—you're more focused, disciplined, and motivated than ever before. This wasn't just a reset; it was a foundation for a lifestyle that thrives on progress and resilience. Remember: **stay hungry, stay reckless, and never stop leveling up.** The journey continues— go crush it! 🚀

5-Day Body Reset Challenge: Days 21–25

Day 21: The New Normal

Workout

- **Warm-Up:** 5 minutes of light cardio (jumping jacks, jogging in place).
- **Circuit (3 rounds):**
  - Push-Ups with a Clap (or regular push-ups) – 12 reps
  - Jump Squats (15 reps)
  - Plank with Shoulder Taps (30 seconds)
  - High Knees (30 seconds)
- **Cool-Down:** Stretch for 5 minutes, focusing on quads and shoulders.

Meal Plan

- **Breakfast:** Overnight Protein Oats with Banana and Chia Seeds (Chapter 4)
- **Lunch:** Shredded Chicken Power Bowl with Lemon-Garlic Dressing (Chapter 3)
- **Dinner:** Spicy Sriracha Salmon with Roasted Veggies (Chapter 6)
- **Snack:** High-Protein Peanut Butter Cups (Chapter 10)

Challenge Task

Evaluate your routine: What's **easy to sustain** and what still feels challenging? Write down one strategy to make the hard parts easier and commit to applying it this week.

Day 22: Level Up

Workout

- **Warm-Up:** 5 minutes of mobility drills (hip circles, arm swings).
- **Strength Circuit (3 rounds):**
  - Bodyweight Deadlifts (15 reps)
  - Side Plank with Reach Under (30 seconds per side)
  - Jump Lunges (12 reps per leg)
  - Flutter Kicks (30 seconds)
- **Cool-Down:** Stretch and foam roll, focusing on hamstrings and lower back.

Meal Plan

- **Breakfast:** Protein Pancakes with Almond Butter Drizzle (Chapter 4)
- **Lunch:** Turkey Taco Lettuce Wraps (Chapter 7)
- **Dinner:** Big Batch Beef & Sweet Potato Hash (Chapter 6)
- **Snack:** Greek Yogurt with a Sprinkle of Cinnamon and Walnuts (Chapter 7)

Challenge Task

Write down one **personal strength** you've discovered during this challenge. Whether it's discipline, resilience, or improved confidence, celebrate it and think about how you can apply it to other areas of your life.

Day 23: Stay Consistent

Workout

- **Warm-Up:** 5 minutes of light cardio (jump rope, jogging).
- **Circuit (3 rounds):**
  - Push-Ups to Failure
  - Jump Squats (12 reps)
  - Bicycle Crunches (30 seconds)
  - Mountain Climbers (30 seconds)
- **Cool-Down:** Gentle stretching for 5 minutes, focusing on quads and shoulders.

Meal Plan

- **Breakfast:** Sweet Potato Protein Pancakes with Honey Drizzle (Chapter 4)
- **Lunch:** Chili-Lime Chicken Bowl (Chapter 6)
- **Dinner:** Protein-Packed Veggie Stir-Fry (Chapter 7)
- **Snack:** Protein Mug Cake with a Sprinkle of Dark Chocolate Chips (Chapter 10)

Challenge Task

Reflect on your **biggest challenges** during this reset. Write down how you've overcome them and what that says about your ability to tackle future obstacles.

Day 24: Keep Pushing

Workout

- **Warm-Up:** 5 minutes of dynamic stretches.
- **Circuit (4 rounds):**
    - Burpees (15 reps)
    - Bodyweight Squats (20 reps)
    - Plank with Hip Dips (30 seconds)
    - High Knees (30 seconds)
- **Cool-Down:** Foam rolling and deep breathing for 5 minutes.

Meal Plan

- **Breakfast:** Beast Mode Breakfast Bowl (Chapter 3)
- **Lunch:** Protein Nachos with Lean Turkey and Fresh Salsa (Chapter 10)
- **Dinner:** One-Pan Lemon Garlic Salmon with Steamed Broccoli (Chapter 6)
- **Snack:** Greek Yogurt Ranch Dip with Veggie Sticks (Chapter 7)

Challenge Task

Think ahead to **your next big goal**. Write down what you'll focus on after this challenge—whether it's building strength, improving endurance, or mastering your nutrition. Break it into **actionable steps.**

Day 25: Finish Stronger Than Ever

Workout

- **Warm-Up:** 5 minutes of light cardio.
- **Final Challenge (4 rounds):**
    - Burpees (20 reps)
    - Push-Ups with Hold at the Bottom (10 reps)
    - Bodyweight Deadlifts (20 reps)
    - Plank Hold (1 minute)
- **Cool-Down:** Full-body stretch, focusing on hamstrings, shoulders, and lower back.

Meal Plan

- **Breakfast:** Overnight Protein Oats with Fresh Strawberries (Chapter 4)

- **Lunch:** Shredded Chicken Salad with Avocado Dressing (Chapter 3)
- **Dinner:** Cauliflower Crust Pizza with Veggie and Turkey Toppings (Chapter 10)
- **Snack:** Creamy Avocado Protein Smoothie (Chapter 7)

Challenge Task

Reflect on your **entire 25-day journey**. Write down:

1. **The biggest change** you've noticed—physically, mentally, or both.
2. **Your proudest moment** during the challenge.
3. **What's next**—how will you maintain and build on your progress?

Final Words

You've conquered 25 days of focused effort, discipline, and grit. This isn't just the end of a challenge—it's the start of a lifestyle. Use the momentum you've built to tackle bigger goals, push harder, and stay hungry for more. You're unstoppable now—so go out there and keep crushing it. **Stay reckless. Stay hungry. Keep dominating.** 🚀

5-Day Body Reset Challenge: Days 26–30

Day 26: Test Your Limits

Workout

- **Warm-Up:** 5 minutes of light cardio (jump rope, jogging).
- **Circuit (4 rounds):**
    - Burpees with a Tuck Jump (10 reps)
    - Push-Ups to Failure
    - Jump Lunges (10 reps per leg)
    - Plank with Shoulder Taps (30 seconds)
- **Cool-Down:** Stretch for 5 minutes, focusing on hips and shoulders.

Meal Plan

- **Breakfast:** Sweet Potato Protein Pancakes with a Drizzle of Honey (Chapter 4)
- **Lunch:** Chili-Lime Chicken Bowl (Chapter 6)
- **Dinner:** Spicy Sriracha Salmon with Steamed Asparagus (Chapter 6)
- **Snack:** High-Protein Cheesecake Cups (Chapter 10)

Challenge Task

Write down one thing you **never thought you'd accomplish** during this challenge—and then think about what else you're capable of. Let this moment expand your belief in your potential.

Day 27: Reclaim Your Energy

Workout

- **Warm-Up:** 5 minutes of mobility drills (hip circles, arm swings).
- **Circuit (3 rounds):**
    - Push-Ups with Hold at the Bottom (12 reps)
    - Bodyweight Deadlifts (15 reps)
    - High Knees (30 seconds)
    - Flutter Kicks (30 seconds)
- **Cool-Down:** Foam roll or yoga stretches for 5 minutes.

Meal Plan

- **Breakfast:** Overnight Protein Oats with Almond Butter (Chapter 4)
- **Lunch:** Shredded Chicken Salad with Avocado Dressing (Chapter 3)
- **Dinner:** Protein-Packed Veggie Stir-Fry (Chapter 7)
- **Snack:** Greek Yogurt with Dark Chocolate Chips (Chapter 7)

Challenge Task

Take 15 minutes to **visualize your future self**. How do they move, think, and perform? Write down three traits you admire in that version of you and commit to embodying them now.

Day 28: Refocus on Strength

Workout

- **Warm-Up:** 5 minutes of light cardio.
- **Strength Circuit (4 rounds):**
    - Bodyweight Squats (20 reps)
    - Push-Ups with a Clap (10 reps)
    - Side Plank Holds (30 seconds per side)
    - Mountain Climbers (30 seconds)
- **Cool-Down:** Gentle stretching for 5 minutes, focusing on hamstrings and shoulders.

Meal Plan

- **Breakfast:** Beast Mode Breakfast Bowl (Chapter 3)
- **Lunch:** Turkey Taco Lettuce Wraps with Salsa (Chapter 7)
- **Dinner:** Big Batch Beef & Sweet Potato Hash (Chapter 6)
- **Snack:** Peanut Butter Protein Bars (Chapter 10)

Challenge Task

List three things that **used to feel hard** at the start of this challenge that now feel easy. Recognize how much stronger and more capable you've become.

Day 29: Prove Your Progress

Workout

- **Warm-Up:** 5 minutes of dynamic stretches.
- **Circuit (3 rounds):**
    - Burpees with a Tuck Jump (12 reps)
    - Bodyweight Deadlifts (15 reps)
    - Jump Squats (15 reps)
    - Plank Hold (1 minute)
- **Cool-Down:** Foam roll or stretch for 5 minutes.

Meal Plan

- **Breakfast:** Protein Pancakes with Peanut Butter and Banana Slices (Chapter 4)
- **Lunch:** Chili-Lime Chicken Bowl (Chapter 6)
- **Dinner:** One-Pan Lemon Garlic Salmon with Steamed Veggies (Chapter 6)
- **Snack:** Protein Mug Cake with Greek Yogurt (Chapter 10)

Challenge Task

Write a letter to your future self. Share the lessons you've learned, the wins you've had, and the determination you've built. Seal it and open it a month from now to remind yourself how far you've come.

Day 30: Finish Like a Legend

Workout

- **Warm-Up:** 5 minutes of light cardio or dynamic stretches.
- **Final Challenge (4 rounds):**
    - Burpees with Tuck Jump (15 reps)
    - Push-Ups to Failure
    - Jump Lunges (12 reps per leg)
    - Plank with Shoulder Taps (1 minute)
- **Cool-Down:** Full-body stretch, focusing on quads, hamstrings, and shoulders.

Meal Plan

- **Breakfast:** Overnight Protein Oats with Fresh Strawberries and Chia Seeds (Chapter 4)

- **Lunch:** Shredded Chicken Power Bowl with Lemon Dressing (Chapter 3)
- **Dinner:** Cauliflower Crust Pizza with Veggie and Turkey Toppings (Chapter 10)
- **Snack:** Creamy Avocado Protein Smoothie (Chapter 7)

Challenge Task

Reflect on the entire 30-day challenge. Write down:

1. **Your biggest accomplishments.**
2. **The most valuable lessons learned.**
3. **Your next steps**—how will you build on this momentum?

You've just crushed 30 days of focused, intentional effort. Every workout, every recipe, every decision has been a step toward a stronger, more disciplined version of yourself. But let's be real—this isn't just about 30 days. It's about what comes next. You've proven that you can do hard things, that you can stick with it, and that you're capable of more than you thought.

This isn't the finish line—it's just the **next step in your relentless journey.** Keep showing up, keep pushing, and stay hungry for greatness. You've got this. Let's go.

The Final Word: Your New Reckless Life

You made it. Not just through this book, but through the **process of transformation.** From the first recipe to the last workout, every chapter, every bite, every rep was designed to push you out of your comfort zone and into the realm of **unstoppable.**

Let's be clear: this isn't just about how much protein you packed into your breakfast or how many burpees you crushed during a circuit. Those are tools—**weapons**, really. The real win here? You've unlocked a mindset that most people never even dream of. You're no longer just chasing goals—you're **living the process**, and that's where the real power lies.

You're Not Done, and That's the Point

You've built something here. Something bigger than abs, bigger than PRs, bigger than any single milestone. You've built the foundation for a **lifestyle of relentless growth**. You've learned to embrace discipline, to crush excuses, and to push past plateaus like they were speed bumps. But here's the kicker: you're not done. You never will be.

Because this isn't the end of your journey—it's the launchpad. Every recipe you've mastered, every habit you've formed, every rep you've gritted through has been about one thing: **building momentum.** And momentum doesn't stop. It grows. It snowballs. It pulls you forward into your next victory, your next challenge, your next version of yourself.

What Happens Next?

You already know the answer. You keep going.

- When the workouts get boring? You level up.
- When the meals feel routine? You experiment.
- When life throws curveballs? You adapt and keep moving forward.

You don't stop. You don't settle. You don't make excuses. Why? Because you've proven to yourself that you don't need them. You've proven that you're capable of more than you thought, and the only limit now is the one you're willing to set. **And let's be real—you're not about limits.**

A Reminder for the Reckless

The world is full of people who are **comfortable with mediocrity.** They take shortcuts. They settle for less. They complain about why they can't while you're out there proving that you can. Let them stay in their lane while you redefine what's possible for yourself. You're not reckless because you're careless—you're reckless because you refuse to accept anything less than **extraordinary.**

One Last Push

Before you close this book, make a promise to yourself. A promise to keep the fire burning, to keep pushing when it feels impossible, to wake up every day hungry for more. Whether it's crushing your next workout, nailing your macros, or just being 1% better than you were yesterday, **you owe it to yourself to show up.**

This book isn't just a guide—it's a contract. A contract with the version of you that refuses to back down, that thrives on the grind, that chases greatness like it's oxygen. Sign it. Live it. **Own it.**

Stay Hungry. Stay Reckless. Keep Dominating.

This isn't goodbye. It's just the end of this chapter and the start of something bigger. Go out there and show the world what happens when you stop making excuses and start making progress. You've got the tools, the mindset, and the drive. Now, **go dominate.**

Let's go.